Contents

Background

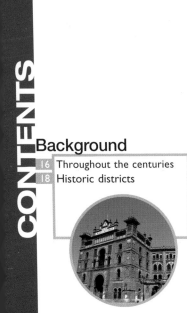

The Paseo del Arte

Exploring the city

Highlights

Excursions

Directory

Index

3

Madrid is one of Europe's most hospitable, cosmopolitan and lively cities, with wide avenues, attractive parks and a great sense of joie de vivre. The enchantment of Old Madrid, the extraordinary collections in the museums, among the world's finest, the magnificent monuments, the beautiful avenues and lovely parks are just some of the attractions the city offers to visitors.

In addition, Madrid is famed for lively, intense nightlife. Nights here go on till dawn, and there is plenty of entertainment for all tastes.

While proud of its past, Madrid is most certainly a modern capital on the move, its urban environment and its inhabitants always up-to-date. It is a city open to the world.

J. Malburet/MICHELIN

Introduction

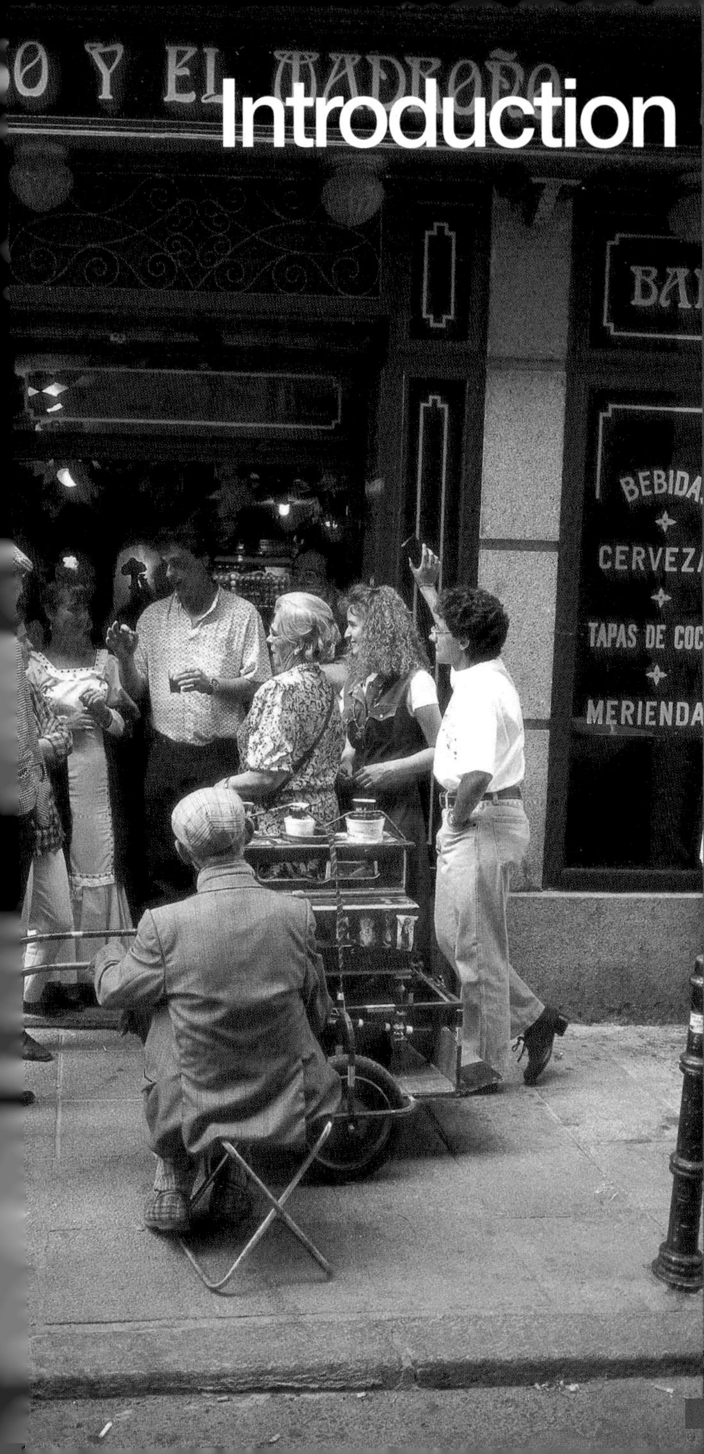

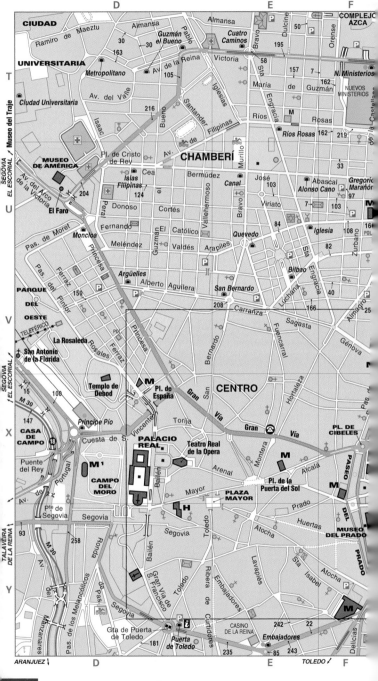

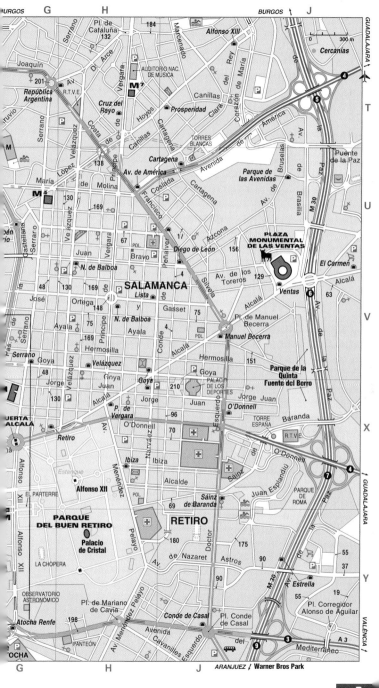

J. Martín Márquez/MICHELIN

Jardín Botánico

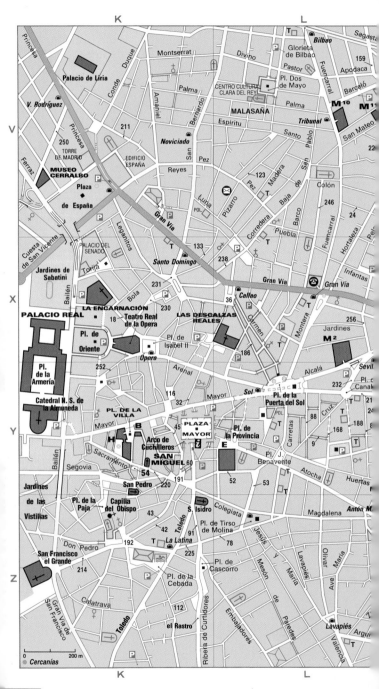

MADRID

Population: 3 084 673. Michelin maps 575 or 576 K 18-19 (town plan) – map 121 Alrededores de Madrid – Michelin City Plan Madrid 42 and 2042 – Madrid.

Europe's highest capital stands at an altitude of 646m/2 119ft at the centre of the Iberian Peninsula, to the southeast of the Sierra de Guadarrama mountain range. The city has a dry, continental climate characterised by hot summers and cold, sunny winters. Madrid is a very accessible city, easily reached by air, rail or road. Because traffic is heavy and it is difficult to park – especially in Old Madrid –, we advise you to use public transport within the city. The metro is very modern, and the quickest way to get from one place to another; buses provide a good vantage point for seeing the city. Madrid is a good city for walking too, so don't hesitate to set off on foot, enjoying a stroll under the sparkling blue skies that are emblematic of the capital.

🖪 Plaza Mayor 3, 28013 Madrid, ☏ 91 588 16 36; Duque de Medinaceli 2, 28014 Madrid, ☏ 91 429 49 51/31 77; Madrid-Barajas Airport, 28042 Madrid, ☏ 91 305 86 56. www.munimadrid.es

J. Malburet/MICHELIN

Location

La Gran Vía seen from Calle de Alcalá

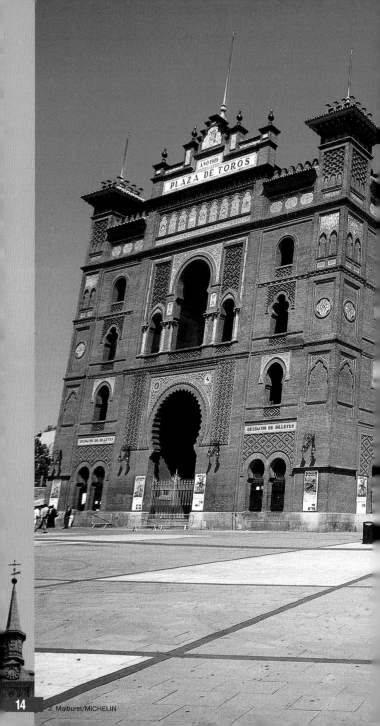

Background

Throughout the centuries

Madrid in the past

Madrid, an unimportant village until the Moorish invasion, owes its name to the fortress (alcázar) of Majerit built during the rule of Mohammed I on the banks of the Manzanares in the 9C. In 1083 it was captured by Alfonso VI, who, it is said, discovered a statue of the Virgin by a granary (almudín) as he entered the town. He then converted the town mosque into a church, dedicating it to the Virgin of the Almudena who was declared the city patron. From the 14C the kings of Castilla came regularly to Madrid; Emperor Charles V rebuilt the Muslim alcázar and in 1561 Philip II moved the court from Toledo to Madrid. The medieval town expanded rapidly and the population tripled (at the time of the king's death, there were 60,000 people living in Madrid). Its layout of winding streets can still be seen today around Plaza Mayor.

The town really began to develop under the last of the Habsburgs, in the middle of Spain's Golden Age (16C). During the reign of Philip III, Juan Gómez de Mora undertook a series of reforms and from then on Plaza Mayor was to be the heart of the city. The town plan drawn up in 1656 by Pedro Texeira, gives a good impression of Madrid under Philip IV, when it had a large number of convents and churches. The king was an art lover who gave his patronage to many artists including Velázquez and Murillo, as well as men of letters such as Lope de Vega, Quevedo, Calderón and Tirso de Molina.

From a town to a city

It was in the 18C under the Bourbons that the town underwent its greatest transformations. Philip V decided to build a royal palace, and Charles III, inspired by ideas from European courts, provided Madrid with splendour hitherto unknown. This was the Prado and the Puerta de Alcalá, magnificent examples of neo-Classical town planning. In turn, the nobility began building **palaces**, such as **Liria** and **Buenavista**, which they surrounded with gardens.

The 19C began with occupation by the French and the Madrid rebellion of May 1808 and the brutal reprisals it provoked. In the second half of the 19C, Madrid underwent great alteration: in 1857 the remaining ramparts were demolished and a vast expansion plan (ensanche) gave rise to the districts of Chamberí, Salamanca and Argüelles, and, at the end of the century,

Arturo Soria's *Ciudad Lineal*, a revolutionary town planning project.

At the beginning of the 20C, architecture was French-inspired, as can be seen in the Ritz and Palace hotels; the neo-Mudéjar style was also popular and brick façades so characteristic of Madrid went up all over the city. The Gran Vía, a busy thoroughfare which crosses the centre of town to link Madrid's new districts, was inaugurated in 1910 and has since been popularised in an operetta *(zarzuela)*.

Madrid today

As capital, Madrid is Spain's leading city as far as banks, insurance companies, universities, administrative bodies and political institutions are concerned. It is also an important industrial and technological centre.

The business district, centred around the Puerta de Alcalá and paseo de la Castellana, was modified extensively between 1950 and 1960 when traditional mansions were demolished to make room for new buildings. The city's most modern edifices may be seen in the **AZCA** area, the result of one of Madrid's most revolutionary projects, designed to fulfil various administrative, residential and commercial functions. Among its most noteworthy buildings are the avant-garde **Banco de Bilbao-Vizcaya** and the **Torre Picasso**.

Puerta de Alcalá

Historic districts

Madrid is an enchanting city. It opens itself to visitors like the petals of a flower, gently unfolding and blooming into quaint streets, wide plazas and a collection of distinctive neighbourhoods.

Centro

This district is made up of several areas, each with its own individual character. It has a reputation for being noisy, chaotic and full of people, although visitors are often surprised by its narrow alleyways and small squares. **Sol-Callao** is the shopping area par excellence, packed with locals and visitors out for a stroll, heading for the main pedestrian precinct (Preciados district) or for a drink or dinner in one of the many local cafés and restaurants. A number of cinemas are also located in this area. Visitors should take particular care in the evening, especially in streets such as Valverde and Barco.

Barrio de los Austrias

Madrid's oldest district is wedged between calles Mayor, Bailén, Las Cavas and the plaza de la Cebada. Its origins are medieval and it still retains its evocatively named streets and Mudéjar towers. An excellent area for tapas, dinner or a drink. On Sundays, the famous **Rastro** flea market is held nearby (see p 48).

Lavapiés

This district is located around the square of the same name with many houses dating from the 17C. It is considered to be Madrid's most colourful district with a mix of locals, students and a large immigrant population.

Huertas

Huertas was home to the literary community in the 17C and the Movida movement in the 1980s. Nowadays, it is packed with bars and restaurants and is particularly lively at night, attracting an interesting mixture of late-night revellers.

Malasaña

This part of Madrid, which used to be known as Maravillas, is situated between Las glorietas de Bilbao y Ruiz Jiménez and around plaza del Dos de Mayo. In the mornings, this 19C *barrio* is quiet and provincial, but it is transformed at night by the legions of young people heading towards Malasaña's many bars. For those in search of a quieter night out, the district also has a number of more tranquil cafés.

Alonso Martínez

The average age and financial standing of this district's inhabitants is somewhat higher than in neighbouring Bilbao and Malasaña, as shown by the myriad upmarket bars and restaurants frequented by the city's rich and famous.

Chueca

This district covers an area around the plaza de Chueca; its approximate outer limits are the paseo de Recoletos, calle Hortaleza, Gran Vía and calle Fernando VI. At the end of the last century it was one of Madrid's most elegant districts. Today it is the city's gay area with a multitude of small and sophisticated boutiques.

Salamanca

In the 19C, Salamanca was Madrid's principal bourgeois district designed by the Marquis of Salamanca in the shape of a draughts board with wide streets at right angles. Nowadays, the district is one of the capital's most expensive areas and is home to some of Spain's leading designer boutiques (Serrano and Ortega y Gasset) and an impressive collection of stores selling luxury goods.

The Bear and the Strawberry Tree, Puerta del Sol

HOTEL
UROP

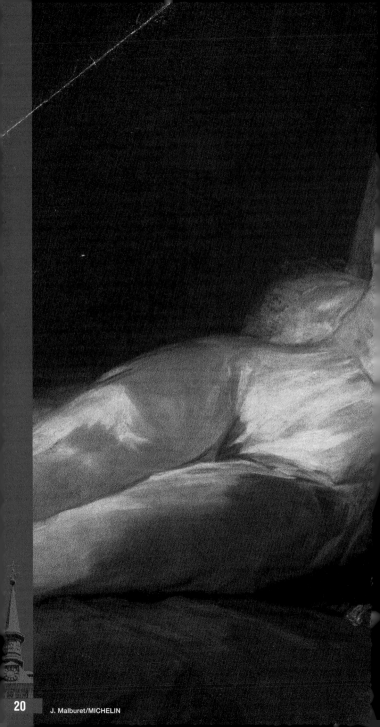

The Paseo
del Arte

La Maja vestida, Goya. Museo del Prado

Museo del Prado ★★★

The Prado is probably the greatest gallery of Classical paintings in the world. The neo-Classical building was designed by Juan de Villanueva under Charles III to house the Natural Science Museum. After the War of Independence (the Peninsular War), Ferdinand VII altered the project and instead installed the collections of Spanish painting made by the Habsburg and Bourbon kings, which reflect the development of royal artistic taste over the centuries. The Prado also contains precious collections of work by Flemish painters, acquired by the Catholic Monarchs, as well as a great many paintings from the Italian School favoured by Emperor Charles V and Philip II.

VISITING THE PRADO

☎ *91 330 28 00. Open 9am-7pm daily except Mon 9am-7pm.* The museum is currently continuing significant renovation works (cloisters of the church of los Jerónimos, the vestibule, etc.), which were still underway when this book went to press. The Casón del

© TURESPAÑA

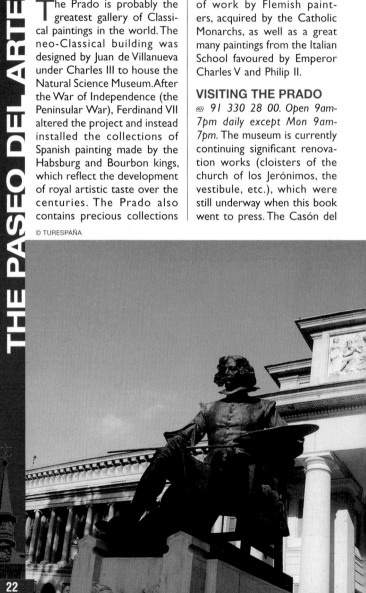

El Paseo del Arte

This poetic name refers to the imaginary axis linking Madrid's three greatest museums (the Prado, Thyssen-Bornemisza and the Reina Sofía), which form a close triangle in the same part of the city. The **Bono Arte**, a combined ticket on sale in each of the museums, entitles the holder to admission to all three of these magnificent art galleries.

Buen Retiro building (calle Alfonso XII, n°28) is closed for renovation.

Given the many important works of art that are kept here, some paintings are only shown during temporary exhibits.

Spanish School★★★
(15C-18C)

Bartolomé Bermejo (*Santo Domingo de Silos* – with his costume rich in gold) and **Yáñez de la Almedina**, who developed the style and technique of Leonardo (*Santa Catalina*), stand out as two painters who cultivated an international style. Masip and his son **Juan de Juanes** (*The Last Supper*) are more associated with the style of Raphael, while Morales' favourite subject, a *Virgin and Child*, is also outstanding.

In those rooms devoted to the **Golden Age**, two painters stand out: **Sánchez Coello**, a disciple of the portrait painter Antonio Moro, and his pupil **Pantoja de la Cruz**, who was another portraitist at the court of Philip II. The personal-

Museo del Prado, statue of Velázquez

ity of **El Greco**, who followed strong Byzantine traditions during his studies in Venice, stands apart within the Spanish School. Here, works dating from his early Spanish period (*Trinity*) through to his maturity (*Adoration of the Shepherds*) can be seen and the evolution of his style studied. Other works are proof that he was a great portraitist; pay particular note to the *Gentleman with his Hand on his Breast*. **Ribalta** is the Spanish Baroque artist who first introduced tenebrism to Spain with its chiaroscuro technique already seen in Caravaggio's work. **José (Jusepe) de Ribera**, also known as **Lo Spagnoletto**, is represented by his major work, the *Martyrdom of St Felipe* – which was originally thought to be of St Bartholomew – in which the artist's vigorous use of chiaroscuro emphasises the dramatic, horrifying nature of the scene. Both the portraits and still-life paintings of **Zurbarán** are peaceful compositions in which the use of chiaroscuro and realism are triumphant. In the Prado we discover the lesser known aspect of the style of this "Painter of Monks", both in the series of *The Labours of Hercules* which he painted for the Casón del Buen Retiro and in the portrait of *St Isabel of Portugal*. **Murillo**, who mainly painted Marian religious scenes, also cultivates popular subjects with delightful realism; note his enchanting child portraits (*The Good Shepherd* and The Boys of the Shell).

Velázquez (1599-1660) – The Prado possesses the greatest paintings of Velázquez. This artist of genius, born in Sevilla, was apprenticed first to Herrera the Elder and then to Francisco Pancheco whose daughter he married in 1618. He later moved to Madrid where he was called to the court by Philip IV in 1623 and subsequently painted a great many portraits. On the suggestion of Rubens he spent some time in Italy (1629-31) where he painted **The Forges of Vulcan**. Influenced by Titian and Tintoretto he began to use richer, more subtle colours and developed his figure compositions as can be seen in his magnificent **Christ on the Cross**. On his return he painted **The Surrender of Breda** in which his originality emerges and where, as is borne out by the composition, the emphasis rests on the psychological relationship between the protagonists. The use of light in his pictures is crucial, setting off figures and objects yet also giving life to the space between them; on the strength of this Velázquez developed his famous aerial perspectives in which parts of the picture are left hazy in order to further highlight the central figures. He strove towards naturalism, as is shown in his royal hunting portraits of **Philip IV** and **Prince Baltasar Carlos, the Hunter** (1635, a wonderful rendering of a child) and his equestrian portraits of the royal family, in particular that of **Prince Baltasar Carlos on Horseback** with the *sierra* in the background. His predilection for realism is evident in his pictures of Aesop, as well as of buffoons and dwarfs, his favourite themes. In 1650 he returned to Italy where he painted two light, modern landscapes, the

The Prado's Major Works

SCHOOL	ARTIST	PAINTING
Spanish	Juan de Juanes	*Ecce Homo*
16C-18C	El Greco	*Gentleman with his Hand on his Breast*
		Adoration of the Shepherds
	Zurbarán	*Still Life*
		St Isabel of Portugal
	Velázquez	*The Surrender of Breda*
		The Spinners
		The Maids of Honour (Las Meninas)
		Prince Baltasar Carlos on Horseback
		Infanta Doña Margarita of Austria
		The Forges of Vulcan
		Christ on the Cross
	Murillo	*Holy Family with a Little Bird*
		Immaculate Conception of Soult
		The Good Shepherd
	Goya	*Family of Charles IV*
		Maja Naked, Maja Clothed
		Executions at Moncloa
		The Second of May
		The Witches' Coven
Flemish	Robert Campin	*St Barbara*
15C-17C	Van der Weyden	*Deposition*
	Hans Memling	*Adoration of the Magi*
	Bruegel the Elder	*Triumph of Death*
	Hieronymus Bosch	*Garden of Earthly Delights*
	Rubens	*The Three Graces*
Italian	Fra Angelico	*Annunciation*
15C-17C	Andrea Mantegna	*Dormition of the Virgin*
	Botticelli	*Story of Nastagio degli Onesti*
	Titian	*Venus with the Organist*
	Tintoretto	*Washing of the Feet*
	Veronese	*Venus and Adonis*
	Albrecht Dürer	*Self-portrait*
German and Dutch 16C-17C	Rembrandt	*Artemisa*

Gardens of the Villa Medici. During the last years of his life, when he was laden with honours and all manner of official functions, he portrayed the young princes and princesses very freely. In his masterpiece, **The Maids of Honour (Las Meninas)** (1656), a magnificent display of light and colour, the Infanta Margarita is shown in the artist's studio accompanied by her maids and dwarves while the king and queen are portrayed in a mirror in the background. In **The Spinners** (1657), Velázquez has combined myth and reality in a wonderful interplay of oblique lines and curves.

Among the disciples of Velázquez was the court painter **Carreño de Miranda** (*Monstrua Naked* and *Clothed*). Mention should also be made of **Alonso Cano** who painted scenes of the *Immaculate Conception*.

Goya (1746-1828) – Spanish painting maintained its supremacy in the 18C and 19C with Goya (born in Fuentedetodos, Aragón, in 1746), who is magnificently represented in several rooms. His many portraits of the royal and famous, his war scenes, his depiction of everyday life which served as a model for tapestries, and finally his **Majas**, all widely illustrate his extraordinary Realism and his enthusiasm for colour. The museum contains some 40 cartoons painted in oil between 1775 and 1791 for weaving at the Real Fábrica (Royal Tapestry Works). The colourful naturalness of the scenes

gives a delightful picture of life in 18C Madrid. A little further on are the canvases of the **The Second of May** and the **Execution of the Defenders of Madrid on 3 May 1808** painted by Goya in 1818. Here he was inspired by the rebellion in Madrid in 1808 against the French occupying forces when the people wished to prevent the departure of the queen and princes for Bayonne. The reprisal by Murat that ensued was terrible. Goya condemned the horror of that night and the executions that took place on Príncipe Pío hill. The two paintings bring out the violence and cruelty of war as do Goya's brutal etchings of the *Disasters Of War* (1808) and *La Tauromaquia*. The so-called *Black Paintings* (1820-22) on the ground floor, which Goya made for his house, the Quinta del Sordo, are the anguished reactions of a visionary to the reality of life in Spain at the time *(The Witches' Coven, Cronus Swallowing his Son).*

Flemish School★★★ (15C-17C)

The Prado has an exceptional collection of Flemish painting due to the close relations Spain developed with the Low Countries in the past.

Among the Flemish Primitives is the noticeable interest in interiors *(St Barbara* by Robert Campin known as the Master of Flemalle) to which **Van der Weyden** added great richness of colour, a sense of composition and the pathetic *(Descent from the Cross, Pietà).* The dramatic

The Second of May, Goya, the Prado

27

aspect is interpreted differently, through melancholy, by his successor, **Memling** *(Adoration of the Magi)*. There follow the weird imaginings of **Hieronymus Bosch**, known as El Bosco *(The Garden of Earthly Delights)* which influenced his disciple Patinir *(Crossing the Stygian Lake)*, and a painting by **Bruegel the Elder**, the *Triumph of Death*. Notable in the collection of Flemish paintings from the 16C and 17C are **Ambrosius Benson**'s religious pictures, the portraits of personalities at the court of Philip II by the Dutchman, **Antonio Moro** (16C), the series of the *Five Senses* by Brueghel the Younger (17C) and his and **David Teniers the Younger**'s colourful scenes of everyday life.

© TURESPAÑA

The most Baroque of painters, **Rubens** (who was born in Germany), breathed new life into Flemish painting *(The Three Graces)*. There is a rich collection of his work in the museum completed by that of his disciples: **Van Dyck**, excellent portraits, Jordaens, everyday-life scenes, and animal paintings by their contemporaries, Snyders and Paul de Vos.

Dutch School (17C)

There are two interesting works by **Rembrandt**: a *Self-portrait* and *Artemesia*.

Italian School** (15C-17C)

The Italian School is particularly well represented from the 15C and is especially rich in works by Venetian painters.

The Italian Renaissance brought with it elegance and ideal beauty as in paintings by **Raphael** *(The Holy Family, Portrait of a Cardinal)*, Roman nobility and monumental bearing in the work of **Mantegna** *(Dormition of the Virgin)* and melancholic dreaminess in **Botticelli** *(Story of Nastagio degli Onesti)*. On the other hand, the spirituality of the magnificent *Annunciation* by **Fra Angelico** belongs to the Gothic tradition. The collection also includes soft-coloured works by Andrea del Sarto, and others by Correggio, an artist from the Parma School who used *chiaroscuro*.

The triumph of colour and sumptuousness comes with the Venetian school: **Titian** with his exceptional mythological scenes *(Danae and the Golden Shower, Venus with the Organist)* and his admirable portrait of *Emperor Charles V*; **Veronese** with his fine compositions set off by silver tones; **Tintoretto**'s golden-fleshed figures springing from shadow *(Washing of the Feet)* and finally **Tiepolo**'s paintings intended for Charles III's royal palace.

French School (17C-18C)

The French are represented by **Poussin** landscapes and canvases by **Lorrain** (17C).

German School

This is represented by a selection of **Dürer's** figure and portrait paintings *(Self-portrait, Adam and Eve)* and two hunting scenes and a religious canvas by Cranach.

Inside the Prado

Museo Thyssen-Bornemisza★★★

The neo-Classical Palacio de Villahermosa has been magnificently restored by the architect Rafael Moneo to house an outstanding collection acquired by the Spanish State from **Baron Hans Heinrich Thyssen-Bornemisza**. The collection was assembled in the 1920s by his father, Baron Heinrich, and bears witness to what is considered to be one of the largest and most inspired collections ever brought together in the private art world.

© MUSEO THYSSEN/BORNEMISZA, MADRID

VISITING THE MUSEUM

☎ *91 369 01 51. Open 10am-7pm, closed Mon.*

The museum contains approximately 800 works (mainly paintings) from the late 13C to the present day. They are exhibited in chronological order on three floors (the visit should start on the second (top) floor where the collection's oldest exhibits are displayed), and provide an overview of the main schools of European art (Italian, Flemish, German, Dutch, Spanish, French) in-

cluding examples of Primitive, Renaissance, Baroque, Rococo and neo-Classical works. The gallery also devotes space to 19C American painting, the 20C European Romanticism and Realism movements and presents a representative selection from the Impressionist, Post-Impressionist and Expressionist periods. The visit concludes with paintings from both the European and American avant-garde movements.

Second floor

The visit begins with the Italian Primitives *(Gallery 1)*: **Duccio di Buoninsegna**'s *Christ and the Samaritan Woman*, in which concern for scenic realism – one of the predominant themes of the Renaissance – can be seen, stands out. **Gallery 3** displays some splendid examples of 15C Dutch religious painting such as **Jan van Eyck**'s *The Annunciation Diptych*, in which the artist parades his prodigious technique by giving the finely-proportioned Angel and the Virgin the appearance of high reliefs carved in stone; next to it is the small *Our Lady of the Dry Tree* by **Petrus Christus** in which the Virgin and Child symbolise the flowering of the dry tree.

The museum possesses a magnificent **portrait collection**. It is worth spending some time in **Gallery 5** which contains some superb examples of the Early Renaissance which encompass its values of identity and autonomy. These come

to the fore in the beautiful and well-known *Portrait of Giovanna Tornuaboni* by the Italian painter **D Ghirlandaio**. The room also houses a further dozen portraits of exceptional quality which emanate from various schools from the period, notably *A Young Man at Prayer* by **Hans Memling**, *A Stout Man* by **Robert Campin**, *Henry VIII* by **Hans Holbein the Younger** and **Juan of Flanders'** extremely delicate *Portrait of an Infanta (Catherine of Aragón?)*.

Raphael's *Portrait of an Adolescent* can be seen in the Villahermosa Gallery *(Gallery 6)* while **Gallery 7** (16C) reveals **Vittore Carpaccio's** *Young Knight in a Landscape* in which the protagonist's elegance stands out from a background heavy with symbolism. The *Portrait of Doge Francesco Vernier* by **Titian** should not be missed, with its sober, yet diverse tones. After admiring **Dürer's** *Jesus Among the Doctors (Gallery 8)*, where the characters are portrayed in a surprising way given the period (1506), move on to **Gallery 9**, which contains an excellent selection of portraits from the 16C German School including *The Nymph from the Fountain*, one of several paintings by **Lucas Cranach the Elder**, and the *Portrait of a Woman* by **Hans Baldung Grien**, in which the original expression and the delicacy of contrasts give the portrait an attractive air. The display of 16C Dutch paintings in **Gallery 10** includes Patinir's *Landscape with the Rest on the Flight into Egypt* while **Gallery 11** exhibits

several works by **El Greco** as well as **Titian's** *St Jerome in the Wilderness* (1575), with its characteristic use of flowing brushstrokes, painted the year before his death. One of the splendid early works of **Caravaggio** – the creator of tenebrism – *St Catherine of Alexandria*, can be admired in **Gallery 12**. In the same gallery is a splendid sculpture *(St Sebastian)* by Baroque artist **Bernini**, executed at the tender age of 17. Also displayed here is the *Lamentation over the Body of Christ* (1633) by **Ribera** – one of Caravaggio's followers – which captures the Virgin's suffering with great subtlety. After passing through several rooms dedicated to 17C Baroque art (including **Claude Lorrain's** *Pastoral Landscape with a Flight into Egypt* and **Zurbarán's** superb *Santa Casilda*), you reach the 18C Italian Painting section *(Galleries 16-18)* with its typical Venetian scenes by **Canaletto** and **Guardi**. The remaining galleries on this floor *(19-21)* are consecrated to Dutch and Flemish works from the 17C. **Van Dyck's** magnificent *Portrait of Jacques le Roy*, **De Vos'** *Antonia Canis*, and two memorable **Rubens**, *The Toilet of Venus* and *Portrait of a Young Woman with a Rosary*, all hang from the walls of **Gallery 19**, while **Gallery 21** possesses the fine *Portrait of a young Man Reading a Coranto* by **Gerard ter Borch**, skilfully representing the model pictured in his daily environment.

First floor

The first few galleries *(22-26)* represent Dutch paintings from the 17C with scenes of daily life and landscapes. Pay particular

note to **Frans Hals'** *Family Group in a Landscape*, a fine example of a collective portrait. The century is completed by the still-life paintings in **Gallery 27**. Several interesting portraits stand out from the 18C French and British schools, such as **Gainsborough**'s *Portrait of Miss Sarah Buxton* in **Gallery 28**. 19C North-American painting, virtually unknown in Europe, takes pride of place in the next two rooms *(29 and 30)* with works by the Romantic landscape artists Cole, Church, Bierstadt and the Realist Homer. The European Romanticism and Realism of the 19C is best expressed by **Constable**'s *The Lock*, **Courbet**'s *The Water Stream* and **Friedrich**'s *Easter Morning*, together with the three works in the collection by **Goya** *(Gallery 31)*.

Galleries 32 and **33** are dedicated to Impressionism and Post-Impressionism. Here, admire the magnificent works by the principal masters of these movements: Monet, Manet, Renoir, Sisley, Degas, Pissarro, Gauguin, Van Gogh, Toulouse-Lautrec and Cézanne. *At the Milliner* by **Degas** is considered to be one of his major canvases. Other works which equally stand out include **Van Gogh**'s *"Les Vessenots" in Auvers*, a landscape painted in the last year of his life and which displays the explosion of brush-strokes synonymous with some of his later works, *Mata Mua* by **Gauguin**, from his Polynesian period, and **Cézanne**'s *Portrait of a Farmer*, in which his particular use of colour is used

to build volumes, a style which opened the way to Cubism. Expressionism is represented in **Galleries 35-40**, following a small display of paintings from the Fauve movement in **Gallery 34**. The Expressionist movement, the best represented in the entire museum, supposes the supremacy of the artist's interior vision and the predominance of colour over draughtsmanship. The works exhibited illustrate the different focal points of German Expressionism. Two highly emblematic paintings by **Grosz**, *Metropolis* and *Street Scene*, hang in **Gallery 40**.

Ground floor

The first few galleries *(41-44)* contain exceptional Experimental avant-garde works (1907-24) from the diverse European movements: Futurism, Orphism, Suprematism, Constructivism, Cubism and Dadaism. **Room 41** displays Cubist works by **Picasso** *(Man with a Clarinet)*, **Braque** *(Woman with a Mandolin)* and **Juan Gris** *(Woman Sitting)*, while *Proun 1C* by **Lissitzky** and *New York City, New York* by **Mondrian** merit special mention in Room 43.

Gallery 45 shows post-First World War European works by **Picasso** *(Harlequin with a Mirror)* and **Joan Miró** *(Catalan Peasant with a Guitar)*, as well as a 1914 abstract composition by **Kandinsky** *(Picture with Three Spots)*. In the next gallery, mainly dedicated to North American painting, can be seen *Brown and Silver I* by **Jackson Pollock** and *Green on Maroon* by **Mark**

Rothko, two different examples of abstract American Expressionism. The last two galleries *(47 and 48)* are given over to Surrealism, Figurative Tradition and Pop Art. The following are worthy of particular note: *The Key to the Fields* by the Surrealist artist **Réne Magritte**, *Hotel Room* by the Realist Edward Hopper, *Portrait of George Dyer in a Mirror* by **Francis Bacon**, *Express* by **Robert Rauschenberg** and *A Woman in a Bath* by **Roy Lichtenstein**.

Colección Carmen Thyssen-Bornemisza

Since the summer of 2004, visitors can admire the art collection of Baroness Carmen Thyssen-Bornemisza. Shown in a specially designed building, the collection of 250 works of art rounds out the rest of the museum's collection. Paintings from the Dutch School (17C), 18C paintings, Impressionist and Post-Impressionist works are on exhibit as well as German Expressionist works.

MUSEO THYSSEN/BORNEMISZA

Museo Thyssen-Bornemisza

Museo Nacional Centro de Arte Reina Sofía*

The former Hospital de San Carlos was refurbished to house this outstanding museum of contemporary art. The vast arched halls inside form an impressive setting for the programme of temporary cultural exhibitions organised by the centre.

QUEEN SOFIA ART CENTRE
☎ 91 467 50 62. Open 10am-9pm (Sunday 10am-2.30pm); *closed Tue*. After significant work to expand the premises, the new building, designed by Jean Nouvel, was inaugurated in late 2004. It is used for temporary exhibits, while the permanent collection, soon to be enlarged, will be on display on the 3rd floor of the former hospital.

Permanent collection*
This collection is laid out on the second and fourth floors.

J. Martin Márquez/MICHELIN

Oteiza

Avant-garde movements – *Second floor.* The 17 galleries exhibit canvases illustrating leading avant-garde movements in Spanish painting and the international events that prompted them, running from the late 19C to the years following the Second World War.

Some of the galleries cover the work of a single artist. In Gallery 4, which displays Cubist works by the great artist **Juan Gris**, note the remarkable *Portrait of Josette*.

In the gallery devoted to **Picasso** *(GalleryGallery 6)*, one is strongly impressed by *Guernica****, commissioned for the Spanish Pavilion at the 1937 World Fair. Inspired by the terrible bombing of Guernica and much commented on because of its expressiveness and powerful symbolism, this monumental black and white picture is a stark denunciation of the atrocities of war. Gallery 7 shows a retrospective of the work of **Joan Miró**, with *Snail, Woman, Flower, Star* (1934) and *Woman, Bird and Star (Tribute to Picasso)* (1970); his sculptures can be seen in Gallery 16.

There are lovely sculptures by **Julio González** (1920-40s) in Gallery 8. **Dalí** is represented in Gallery 10, where you can admire some

Façade of the Museo Nacional Centro de Arte Reina Sofía

of his early works (*Little Girl at the Window* – 1925), together with later examples taken from his Surrealist period (*The Great Masturbator*).

Post-Civil War movements – *Fourth floor (Rooms 18 to 45).*

Here you can see works reflecting major artistic movements from the late 1940s to the early 1980s. Gallery 19 displays works by artists belonging to **Dau al Set** and **Pórtico**, the two main trends to have emerged in Spain in the wake of the Civil War. Rooms 20 to 23 cover the Abstract movement spanning the 1950s and the early 1960s, illustrated by Guerrero, Ràfols Casamada, Hernández Mompó, Oteiza, Sempere, Palazuelo and members of the **Equipo Crónica**. Informalism is extremely well represented in Rooms 27 to 29 with a fine collection of paintings, divided into those associated with **El Paso** (Millares, Saura, Rivera, Canogar, Feito and Viola) or with the **Cuenca Group** (Zóbel and Torner). An interesting selection of works by **Tàpies** can be seen in Rooms 34 and 35. Figurative art is shown in Gallery 31 with canvases by Antonio López García, Julio López Hernández and Xavier Valls.

In the next gallery, collages taken from the series *Gravi-*

tations of **Eduardo Chillida** accompany his sculpture *Omar Khayyan II's Table* (1983). The works of Alfaro, Arroyo, Luis Gordillo and the Equipo Crónica *(Rooms 36 to 39)* demonstrate the similarities and differences between Pop Art and figurative, narrative works.

In Galleries 42 and 43, the collages from the series Gravitations, by Eduardo Chillida are on exhibit alongside a few of his sculptural works, including The Table of Omar Khayyan II (1983) and Hommage to San Juan de la Cruz. The works of North American artists from the period 1960-1970, such as D. Judd, B. Nauman, B. Newman and E. Kelly, can be seen in **Gallery 41**. The retransmission of images on a screen, characteristic of 20C art, is found in Gallery 44.

The tour of the permanent collection finishes with a selection of works of Spanish and international art from recent decades (Galleries 40 and 45) showing the diversity of current artistic expression: figurative (Barceló, García Sevilla, Katz, Kuitca, etc.), abstract: (Broto, Sicilia, Uslé, Ritcher, Lasker, etc.) and also sculpture, monumental installations (Navarro, Iglesias, Kapoor, Schlosser …) and photography.

Guernica, P. Picasso. Museo Nacional Centro de Arte Reina Sofía, Madrid

J. Malburet/MICHELIN

Exploring the city

Equestrian statue of Philip III, Plaza Mayor

Old Madrid*

Steep, narrow streets, small squares, 17C palaces and mansions, houses with wrought-iron balconies dating from the 19C and early 20C provide the backdrop to this walk through Old Madrid, the very heart of the city, which first developed around plaza Mayor and plaza de la Villa.

It is best to take this walk early in the morning or in the late afternoon, when the churches are open.

Plaza Mayor**

This was built by Juan Gómez de Mora during the reign of Philip III (1619) and forms the architectural centre of **Habsburg Madrid**.

On the north side, flanked by pinnacled towers, stands the **Casa de la Panadería** (a former bakery) which was reconstructed by Donoso in 1672. Its mural decoration, the third since it was built, is the work of the artist Carlos Franco. The 17C equestrian statue of Philip III in the middle of the square is by Giambologna and Pietro Tacca.

The vast square was the setting for *autos-da-fé*, mounted bullfights, and the proclamations of Kings Philip V, Ferdinand VI and Charles IV. Its present appearance is a result of the work carried out by Juan de Villanueva at the end of the 18C.

A stamp and coin market is held under the arches on Sunday mornings while at Christmas, stalls are set up selling religious and festive decorations. The shops around the square, hatters in particular, have retained their look of yesteryear.

Pass through the **Arco de Cuchilleros** into the street of the same name, fronted by tall, aged houses with convex façades. The **Cava de San Miguel** provides a rear view of the houses which look onto the square and gives an indication of the steep slopes around Plaza Mayor. The name *cava* derives from the ditches or moats that once stood here. This area is crowded with small restaurants *(mesones)* and bars *(tavernas)*. The **Mercado de San Miguel**, an indoor market built early this century, has preserved its elegant iron structure.

Head down the calle Conde de Miranda, cross the pleasant plaza del Conde de Barajas and the calle de Gómez de Mora to get to plaza de San Justo or Puerta Cerrada, an old city gate. Continue right along the calle de San Justo.

Iglesia Pontificia de San Miguel*

Open 11.15am-12.15pm, 1-1.30 pm, 6-7pm and 7.30-8.30pm. Closed Sun and public hols. ☎ 91 548 40 11.

The basilica by Bonavia is one of the rare Spanish churches to have been inspired by 18C Italian Baroque. Its convex façade, designed as an interplay of inward and outward curves, is adorned with fine statues. Above the doorway is a low relief of St Justus and St Pastor to whom the basilica was previously dedicated. The interior is graceful and elegant with an oval cupola, intersecting ribbed vaulting, flowing cornices and abundant stuccowork.

Follow calle Puñonrostro – to the left of the church – and calle del Codo, in former times one of Madrid's most dangerous streets because of its reputation for drunkards, to plaza de la Villa.

Plaza de la Villa★

The quiet pedestrian square is presided over by a statue of Álvaro de Bazán, hero of Lepanto, by Benlliure (1888). Several famous buildings are arranged around the square including the **Ayuntamiento** (town hall), built by Gómez de Mora in 1617, the **Torre de los Lujanes** (Lujan Tower), one of the rare examples of 15C civil architecture preserved in Madrid and in which Francis I was imprisoned after the battle of Pavia, and the **Casa de Cisneros**, built several years after the death of the cardinal of the same name, which is connected to the

© TURESPAÑA

Plaza Mayor

Ayuntamiento .....BY **H**
Casa de Pedro Calderón
de la Barca ......BY **D**

Iglesia Arzobispal
Castrense .... AY **F**

Ayuntamiento by an arch. Of the original 16C edifice only an attractive window giving onto plazuela del Cordón remains.

Calle Mayor

The name of this street, literally Main Street, gives us an indication of its historical importance. It has preserved several interesting buildings such as n° 61, the narrow house in which the 17C playright, **Pedro Calderón de la Barca**, lived. The Antigua Farmacia de la Reina Madre (Queen Mother's Pharmacy), close by, has preserved a collection of old chemist's jars and pots.

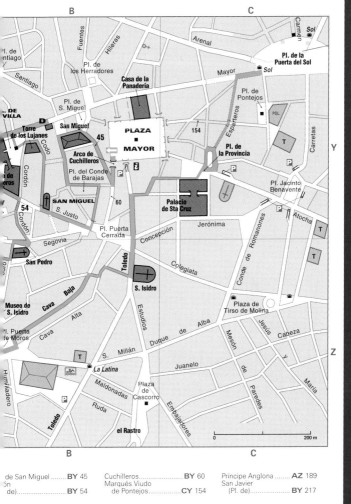

The **Instituto Italiano de Cultura** (n°86) occupies a palace dating from the 17C which has undergone more recent restoration. The Palacio Uceda opposite, a building dating from the same period, is now the military headquarters of the **Capitanía General** (Captaincy General). This brick and granite palace is a fine example of civil architecture of the time.

In front of the **Iglesia Arzobispal Castrense** (17C-18C) is a monument commemorating the attack on Alfonso XIII and Victoria Eugenia on their wedding day in 1906. In the nearby calle de San Nicolás, the Mudéjar tower of San Nicolás de los Servitas can still be seen.

Follow calle del Sacramento, which passes behind plaza de la Villa, to plazuela del Cordón.

Plazuela del Cordón

Just before you reach the square, stop to admire the back of the Casa de Cisneros. From the centre of the *plazuela* there is an unusual view of the façade of the Iglesia de San Miguel.

Return to calle del Cordón and continue to calle de Segovia.

Across the street rises the 14C **Mudéjar tower** of the **Iglesia de San Pedro** (Church of St Peter), which, apart from the Torre de San Nicolás, is the only example of the Mudéjar style in Madrid.

Go along calle del Príncipe Anglona to plaza de la Paja.

Plaza de la Paja

This calm, irregularly built square was, along with the plaza de los Carros, the commercial centre of Madrid in the Middle Ages.

The Palacio Vargas, on one side of the square, obscures

P. Orain/MICHELIN

from view the Gothic **Capilla del Obispo**, a chapel built in the 16C by Gutiérrez Carvajal, Bishop of Palencia. Close to it, in plaza de los Carros, is a chapel, the Capilla de San Isidro, part of the Iglesia de San Andrés, built in the middle of the 17C in honour of Madrid's patron saint. The **Museo de San Isidro** (☎ 91 366 74 15), a museum containing a miracle well and a fine Renaissance patio, is situated next to this complex group of religious buildings.

Walk down calle Don Pedro and cross calle de Bailén. The 1st street on the right leads to the gardens.

Jardines de las Vistillas (Vistillas Gardens)

From the part of the gardens closest to the calle Bailén there is a splendid **panorama★**, especially at sundown, of the Sierra de Guadarrama, Casa de Campo, the Catedral de la Almudena and the viaduct.

Iglesia de San Francisco El Grande

☎ 91 365 38 00.

The church's vast neo-Classical façade is by Sabatini but the building itself, a circular edifice with six radial chapels and a large dome 33m/108ft wide,

Plaza de la Villa

is by Francisco Cabezas. The walls and ceilings of the church are decorated with 19C frescoes and paintings except those in the chapels of St Anthony and St Bernardino which date from the 18C. The Capilla de San Bernardino, the first chapel on the north side, contains in the centre of the wall, a St Bernardino of Siena preaching before the king of Aragón (1781), painted by Goya as a young man.

Some of the Plateresque **stalls*** from the Monasterio de El Parral outside Segovia may be seen in the chancel.

Take carrera de San Francisco and Cava Alta back to calle de Toledo.

Calle de Toledo

This is one of the old town's liveliest streets. The popular **El Rastro** flea market sets up in neighbouring streets and along Ribera de Curtidores every Sunday morning and on public holidays. It is best to come early in the morning because it is very crowded by noon. *Visitors should beware of pickpockets here.*

Iglesia de San Isidro – ☎ *91 369 20 37*. The church with its austere façade and twin towers is by the Jesuits Pedro Sánchez and Francisco Bautista. Formerly the church of the Imperial College of the Company of Jesus (1622), it was the cathedral of Madrid from 1885 until 1993. It contains the relics of Madrid's patron saint, Isidro, and those of his wife, Santa María de la Cabeza.

Plaza de la Provincia

Note the well-proportioned façade of the 17C **Palacio de Santa Cruz**, former court prison (Lope de Vega was incarcerated here) and present Ministry for Foreign Affairs. It was from here that prisoners were taken to be executed in the nearby Plaza Mayor.

Puerta del Sol

The itinerary ends at the Puerta del Sol, the liveliest and best-known square in Madrid. It has been a crossroads for historical events in the city over the ages although its present layout only dates back to the 19C. A small monument illustrating Madrid's coat of arms – a bear and an arbutus (strawberry) tree – stands on the point at which calle del Carmen joins the square. In front of this monument is an equestrian statue of Charles III. At its base, the major works for which the king was responsible in the city have been highlighted. The clock on the former post office (now the headquarters of the Presidencia de la Comunidad de Madrid) chimes the traditional 12 strokes at midnight on New Year's Eve. Kilometre Zero, on the ground in front of the building, marks the point from which all the main roads of Spain radiate and distances are measured.

The many streets leading into Puerta del Sol are crowded with small traditional shops with their colourful wood fronts where customers can just as easily find fans and mantillas as cooked delicacies.

Puerta del Sol

Bourbon Madrid ★★

This is the smart, residential part of Madrid with wide tree-lined avenues bordered by opulent-looking buildings, luxurious palaces and former mansions which now house museums. It is a pleasant area to stroll around in between a visit to the Prado and a walk in the Retiro.

Plaza de Cibeles ★

Standing in the centre of the square is one of the emblems of the city and Madrid's most famous fountain, the 18C Cybele, goddess of fertility who rides a lion-drawn chariot.

The square, the nerve centre of the city, stands at the junction of calle de Alcalá, Gran Vía, paseo del Prado and paseo de Recoletos with its continuation, paseo de la Castellana. Many an artist has been inspired to paint the perspectives opening from the square and the impressive buildings surrounding it such as the **Banco de España** (1891), the 18C **Palacio de Buenavista**, now the Minis-

try for Defence, the late-19C **Palacio de Linares**, now the home of the Casa de América, and the **Palacio de Comunicaciones** or Post and Telegraph Office (1919).

Paseo del Prado ★

This fine, tree-lined avenue runs between plaza de Cibeles and plaza del Emperador Carlos V. Heading south from plaza de Cibeles, the road passes the Ministerio de la Marina and Museo Naval *(see description under Worth a Visit)*, before reaching, in the centre of the avenue, the Fuente de Apolo (Apollo's Fountain), designed by Ventura Rodríguez. The **plaza de la Lealtad**, to the left, with its obelisk dedicated to the heroes of the 2 May, is surrounded by seigniorial buildings such as the neo-Classical **La Bolsa** (Stock Exchange) and the emblematic **Hotel Ritz**.

Plaza de Canóvas del Castillo – This square, embellished by the splendid Fuente de Neptuno (Neptune's Fountain), is overlooked by the

PASEO DEL PRADO

With the 18C drawing to a close, Charles III wanted to develop a public area which would be worthy of Madrid's position as capital of Spain and called upon the court's best architects for his project. In an area outside of the city at the time, Hermosilla, Ventura Rodríguez, Sabatini and Villanueva designed, drained, embellished and built a curved avenue with two large fountains, Cybele and Neptune, at each end, and a third, Apollo, in the centre. To complete the project, the **Botanical Gardens**, **Natural History Museum** (now the Museo del Prado) and the **Observatory**, were also built. The result was a perfect combination of the functional and the ornate dedicated to science and the arts. Since the 16C, the paseo del Prado has been a favourite place for Madrileños to meet and to relax. Today, the avenue retains its dignified air, and provides locals and visitors alike with an opportunity to pass judgement on the vision and imagination of Charles III.

TURESPAÑA   **Plaza de Cibeles at night**

Palacio de Villahermosa, a late-18C to early-19C neo-Classical palace that is now home to the **Museo Thyssen-Bornemisza***** *(see description under The Paseo del Arte)*, and the **Hotel Palace**.

Continuing south, the left-hand side of the paseo del Prado between plaza de Neptuno and plaza del Emperador Carlos V is occupied by the Prado Museum and the **Real Jardín Botánico** (Royal Botanical Gardens) ☏ *91 420 04 38*, both projects the work of Juan de Villanueva.

Museo del Prado*** – This neo-Classical building now home to one of the world's finest art museums was built during the reign of Charles III as the headquarters for the Institute of Natural Sciences. However, following the War of Independence (Peninsular War), Ferdinand VII changed the plans and decided to use it to house the art collections belonging to the Spanish Crown *(see museum description under The Paseo del Arte)*.

Plaza del Emperador Carlos V

The impressive glass and wrought-iron façade of **Atocha railway station** dominates this square at the southern end of the paseo. It is well worth looking inside this remodelled station to view the unusual tropical garden created within it, and to catch a glimpse of the AVE – the high-speed train connecting Madrid with Córdoba and Sevilla.

The former **Hospital de San Carlos**, opposite the station, was created by Charles III, although today it houses the **Museo Nacional Centro de Arte Reina Sofía*** *(see description under The Paseo del Arte)*. This imposing granite building with its austere façade is lightened only by the external glass lifts built to provide access to the museum.

Return in the direction of the Jardín Botánico and walk up **cuesta de Claudio Moyano,** renowned for its second-hand booksellers *(while construction is underway in the cuesta de Claudio Moyano neighbourhood, the booksellers' stalls can be found along the paseo del Prado, in front of the Botanical Gardens.)*

Parque del Buen Retiro** (Retiro Park)

Philip IV commissioned the construction of a palace near the **monasterio de los Jerónimos** (of which only the church remains).

It was subsequently destroyed during the Peninsular War and as a result only the building containing the Museo del Ejér-

cito *(see description under Worth a Visit)* and the Casón del Buen Retiro remain. The Duke of Olivares had the palace grounds developed into a park.

The Retiro, bordered to the west by the impressive calle de Alfonso XII as far as the Puerta de Alcalá, is close to the heart of every madrileño. The park, which covers 130ha/321 acres), is a beautiful island of greenery in the middle of the city with dense clumps of trees (La Chopera at the south end), elegant, formal flower-beds (El Parterre at the north end) and a sprinkling of fountains, temples, colonnades and statues.

Beside the lake (Estanque) where boats may be hired, is the imposing **Monumento a Alfonso XII**. Near the graceful **Palacio de Cristal***, in which exhibitions are held, are a pool and a grotto.

Puerta de Alcalá* (Alcalá Arch)

The arch, which stands at the centre of plaza de la Independencia, was built by Sabatini between 1769 and 1778 to celebrate the triumphant entrance of Charles III into Madrid. The perspective from here, particularly at night, is one of the most beautiful in the city, taking in plaza de Cibeles, calle de Alcalá and the start of the Gran Vía.

The lake in El Retiro

Highlights

Palacio Real seen from
the Campo del Moro gardens

Around the Royal Palace★★

Plaza de la Armería

The vast arcaded square is bounded to the south by the incomplete façade of the **Catedral de la Almudena**. This cathedral, which has taken over a century to complete (the first construction project began in 1879), has a neo-Baroque façade which is in complete harmony with the palace and the excessively cold neo-Gothic interior. It was consecrated by Pope John Paul II in 1993.

The view from the west side of the square extends over the Casa de Campo and the Campo del Moro gardens which slope down to the Manzanares river.

Palacio Real★★ (Royal Palace)

☎ 91 454 88 00 ó 91 542 00 03 *(reservations)*.

The best view of the palace, which overlooks the Manzanares river, is from paseo de Extremadura and from the gardens of the **Campo del Moro★**.

The palace, an imposing edifice built by the Bourbons, was the

J. Malburet/MICHELIN

royal family's official residence until 1931. Today, it is run by the Patrimonio Nacional (Spain's National Trust) and used by the king for state receptions.

On Christmas Day in 1734, while the royal family was staying at the Parque del Buen Retiro, a fire burnt the old Habsburg Alcázar to the ground. Philip V replaced it with a new palace, the present edifice, designed originally by the Italian architect Felipe Juvarra. When Juvarra died, work continued under Sacchetti, who modified his plans, and then under Ventura Rodríguez until completion in the reign of Charles III.

It forms a quadrilateral made of Guadarrama granite and white stone, measuring some 140m/459ft on the sides, on a high bossaged base. The upper register, in which Ionic columns and Doric pilasters alternate, is crowned by a white limestone balustrade. Colossal statues of the kings of Spain from Ataulf to Ferdinand VI were originally intended to be placed above this, but under Charles III they were put in Plaza de Oriente and the Retiro gardens.

The north front gives onto the **Jardines de Sabatini**, the west the **Campo del Moro**. **Plaza de la Armería** stands to the south between the west and east wings of the palace. The east façade gives onto **plaza de Oriente**.

Catedral de Nuestra Señora de la Almudena

Palacio* (Palace) – A monumental staircase with a ceiling painted by Giaquinto leads to the Salón de Alabarderos (Halberdier Room), the ceiling of which was painted by Tiepolo. This leads to the **Salón de Columnas** (Column Room) in which the treaty for Spain's membership of the European Community was signed on 12 June 1985, and where royal celebrations and banquets are held. The next room is the **Salón del Trono*** (Throne Room), which was known as the Salón de Reinos (Kingdom Room) in the 18C. It has totally preserved its decoration from the period of Charles III and is resplendent with crimson velvet hangings and a magnificent ceiling painted by

Tiepolo in 1764 symbolising *The Greatness of the Spanish Monarchy*. The consoles, mirrors and gilded bronze lions are of Italian design. The following three rooms were the king's quarters, occupied by Charles III in 1764. The Saleta Gasparini was the king's dining room; only the ceiling painted by Mengs remains from its original, primitive decoration. The Gasparini antechamber, with a ceiling also painted by Mengs, and Goya portraits of Charles IV and Queen María Luisa of Parma, is followed by the **Cámara Gasparini**, covered from floor to ceiling in pure Rococo decoration.

The Salón de Carlos III was the king's bedroom. It was here that he died in 1788.

The decor is from the period of Ferdinand VII. The **Sala de Porcelana** is, along with its namesake in Aranjuez Palace, the masterpiece of the Buen Retiro Porcelain Factory. Official banquets are held in the Alfonso XII **Comedor de Gala** or Banqueting Hall (for 145 guests), which is adorned with 16C Brussels tapestries. Subsequent rooms display various silver objects, table and crystalware used by the monarchs. The two music rooms contain a collection of instruments including several made by **Stradivarius***. In the chapel are frescoes by Corrado Giaquinto and paintings by Mengs *(Annunciation)* and Bayeu *(St Michael the Archangel)*.

The Queen María Cristina rooms display an unusual mix of styles ranging from the Pompeian decor in the Salón de Estucos (Stucco Room) to the neo-Gothic appearance of the Salón de Billar (Billiard Room).

Real Farmacia (Royal Pharmacy) – Several rooms have been redesigned to display a number of 18C-20C jars, including a fine 18C Talavera glass jar. The inside of a distillation room has also been re-created with retorts, glass flasks, scales and distillation equipment.

Real Armería** (Royal Armoury) – The collection of arms and armour put together by the Catholic Monarchs, Emperor Charles V and

Palacio Real

Philip II, is outstanding. The key pieces of the display include Charles V's suit of armour and the weapons and armour belonging to Philip II and Philip III. A vaulted hall in the basement contains an excellent collection of Bourbon shotguns, ranging from those made by Philip V's armourer to the Winchester given to King Alfonso XII by the President of the United States.

Museo de Carruajes Reales* (Royal Carriage Museum) – ☎ *91 542 00 59*. A pavilion built in 1967 in the middle of the **Campo del Moro** winter garden, which commands a good view of the palace, houses the old royal horse-drawn carriages, most of which date from the reign of Charles IV, in the late 18C. Among the exhibits are the late-17C Carroza Negra or Black Coach made of stained beech and ash, and some 18C berlins, including that used by the Marquis of the House of Alcántara. The coronation coach (drawn by eight horses with accompanying footmen), was built in the 19C for Ferdinand VII and still bears marks of the assassination attempt made on Alfonso XIII and his bride, Victoria Eugenia, in May 1906.

Plaza de Oriente

This attractively landscaped square lies between the east façade of the Palacio Real and the main façade of the Teatro Real. It has recently been re-

P. Orain/MICHELIN

designed and is now a pleasant place for a stroll as it is closed to traffic. At the heart of the gardens, decorated with statues of Gothic kings, stands the magnificent equestrian statue of Philip IV, the work of Pietro Tacca (17C).

Teatro Real – This hexagonal neo-Classical building by architect López de Aguacio was inaugurated as an opera house in 1850 for Isabel II. It has two façades each overlooking a square, one the plaza de Oriente and the other the plaza de Isabel II. The building was fully refurbished during the 1990s.

Monasterio de las Descalzas Reales★★

☎ *91 542 00 59*. Although the convent stands in one of the liveliest parts of Madrid, the moment one steps inside, one is taken right back to the 16C.

It was Joanna of Austria, daughter of Emperor Charles V, who founded the convent of Poor Clares here in the palace in which she was born. For two centuries it served as a retreat for nobles who wished to live retired from the world. The nobility heaped gifts upon the order and its rich collection of religious art is now on display in buildings abutting the conventual cloisters.

The magnificent grand **staircase★**, decorated with frescoes, leads to the upper cloister gallery where each of the **chapels** is more sumptuous than its predecessor. Note the figure of

Teatro Real and the Plaza de Oriente

Christ Recumbent by the 16C sculptor Gaspar Becerra.

In the former nuns' dormitory are ten 17C **tapestries**** based on cartoons by Rubens. Other convent treasures include, on the entresol, various portraits of the royal family and a *St Francis* by Zurbarán; in the chapter house, sculptures, a *Dolorosa* and an *Ecce Homo* by Pedro de Mena and a *Magdalene* by Gregorio Hernández; in the **Relicario** (Reliquary Chamber), a great many finely engraved chalices and caskets; and in the picture galleries, works by Titian, Bruegel the Elder and Rubens.

Real Monasterio de la Encarnacióna
(Royal Convent of the Incarnation)

☏ 91 542 00 59. The convent stands on a delightful square of the same name near the former Alcázar with which it was once connected by a passageway. It was founded in 1611 by Margaret of Austria, wife of Philip III, and occupied by Augustinian nuns. The generosity of each successive Spanish monarch may be seen today in its impressive display of art works.

The collection of paintings from the 17C Madrid School is particularly rich and includes the historically interesting *Exchange of Princesses on Pheasant Island* in 1615 by Van der Meulen and a *St John the Baptist* by Ribera.

There is a noteworthy polychrome sculpture of *Christ at the Column* by Gregorio Hernández on the first floor. The **Relicario***, with a ceiling painted by Vicencio Carducci, contains some 1 500 relics. Among the most notable are the Lignum Crucis and the phial containing the blood of St Pantaleon which is said to liquify each year on 27 July.

The church with its sober quasi-Herreran style portal was originally by Gómez de Mora (1611) but was reconstructed by Ventura Rodríguez in the 18C after the fire in the Alcázar.

Plaza de España

Every visitor to Madrid is bound to spend some time on the large esplanade during a tour of the city centre. The monument to Cervantes in the middle of the square, and the figures of Don Quixote and Sancho Panza, appear overwhelmed by the size of the skyscrapers built in the 1950s, in particular the **Torre de Madrid** and the **Edificio España**.

Starting from the square is the **Gran Vía**, a wide avenue lined by shops, cinemas and hotels, and calle Princesa, popular with the young and with students, which leads towards the **Ciudad Universitaria*** (University City).

Moncloa – Casa de Campo district

Museo Cerralbo*
☏ 91 547 36 46.

The museum, installed in a late 19C mansion, displays the collection left to the Spanish State by the Marquis of Cerralbo, a man of letters and patron of the Arts, on his death in 1922.

A wide range of exhibits can be seen in the mansion's rooms and galleries, including an extensive collection of mainly Spanish paintings, furniture, fans, clocks, armour and weaponry, porcelain, archaeological finds, photographs and personal mementoes belonging to the marquis.

Parque del Oeste*
(West Park)

This delightful landscaped garden, extending across slopes overlooking the Manzanares, was designed at the beginning of the 20C. In the southern part, on Príncipe Pío hill, stands the small 4C BC **Egyptian Temple of Debod**. It once stood beside the Nile in Nubia and was rescued from the waters when the Aswan Dam was being built. Note the hieroglyphs on the interior walls.

The **paseo del Pintor Rosales** nearby, stretching northwestwards, acts as a balcony overlooking the park. Its pavilions and pavement cafés command wonderful views of Velázquez-like sunsets.

La Rosaleda, a rose garden, holds flower shows in June.

Casa de Campo*

This extensive park was reafforested under Philip II in 1559 and today is very popular with *madrileños*.

A **teleférico** (cableway) ☏ 91 541 11 18 or 91 541 74 50, offering superb **views** connects the Parque del Oeste with the **Casa de Campo***. Attractions within the confines of the Casa de Campo include a lake, a swimming pool and an **amusement park**. ☏ 91 463 29 00. The **zoo-aquarium**** (☏ 91 512 37 70) here is said to be one of the largest collections of animals anywhere in Europe.

Museo de América*
(Museum of the Americas)
☏ 91 543 94 37.

This archaeological and ethnological museum, which provides a general overview of European ties with the American continent, has brought together historical, geographical, cultural, artistic and religious aspects of the Americas, at the same time retaining the vision of the New World held by Europe since its discovery. Over 2 500 objects are on display on two floors and are accompanied by explanations, maps, models, reconstructions of dwellings etc. Among the exhibits of great historical value on display, the following stand out: the 17C *Conquest of Mexico*, the *Stele of Madrid* (Mayan), the powerful **Treasure of Los Quimbayas*** (Colombian) and two manuscripts, the *Tudela Manuscript* (1553) and the 13C-16C **Cortesano Manuscript*****, one of four remaining Mayan manuscripts in existence and the museum's prized historical work.

Faro de la Moncloa (Moncloa Beacon)

91 544 81 04. Completed in 1992. From its 76m/250ft high **balcony****, there is a wonderful view of Madrid and its surrounding area. To the northeast, the outline of the Sierra Madrileña can be seen.

Museo del Traje

Avenida Juan Herrera, 2. 915 497 150.

This museum has an interesting collection of costumes. As you walk through the rooms, you can see the evolution from traditional 18C clothing to modern dress, including couture pieces by designers such as Mariano Fortuny and Balenciaga.

Martín Márquez/MICHELIN

Interior of the Templo de Debod

Salamanca – Retiro

Museo Arqueológico Nacional** (National Archaeological Museum)

Entrance in calle Serrano.
☎ 91 577 79 12. Founded in 1867 by Queen Isabel II. Since 1895 it has occupied the same building as the **Biblioteca Nacional** (National Library). *Entrée par le paseo de Recoletos.* The archaeological museum is one of the city's most impressive museums and is without doubt the best museum of its type in Spain.

Art préhistorique d'Égypte et de Grèce* – *Galleries 1-18.* The art of the Upper Palaeolithic period is represented by the reproduction, in the garden, of the **Cuevas de Altamira** (Altamira Caves). *La visite de ces salles débute par une introduction sur les origines de l'Humanité.* The arrival of metal in the Iberian Peninsula (around the middle of the 3rd millennium BC) coincided with the development of the Los Millares culture. The galleries that follow are devoted to the Bronze Age (2nd millennium BC); the so-called Bell Beaker and El Argar cultures and the Megalithic culture (Talayots) of the Balearic Islands – note the splendid bronze Costix **bulls***. Several galleries exhibit numerous finds discovered outside of the Iberian peninsula. Gallery 13, dedicated to Ancient Egypt, displays various objects of a mainly funerary nature,

including the sarcophagus of Amenemhat from the 21st Tebas dynasty. Classical Athens (gallery 15) is also represented by the magnificent collection of **Greek vases***, which originate mainly from the collection acquired by the Marquis of Salamanca in Italy.

Iberian and Classical Antiquities* – *Galleries 19-26.* Exhibits in two Iberian galleries illustrate the origin of local techniques and the artistic influence of the Phoenicians, the Greeks and the Carthaginians. The works displayed at the beginning of the section show an Eastern tendency: note the *Lady of Galera*, a 7C BC alabaster figurine flanked by sphinxes, and the terracottas from Ibiza, including the Dama de Ibiza, which perhaps represents the goddess Tanit. The second gallery, where the influence of Carthage is obvious, shows sculpture at a high peak of artistic expression: standing out from the greatest Iberian sculptures is the Lady of Elche, the **Dama de Elche***, a stone bust, with a sumptuous head-dress and corsage. In the same gallery are the **Dama de Baza****, a realistic goddess figure of the 4C BC which has preserved much of its colour, and the woman bearing an offering discovered at Cerro de los Santos. Other galleries illustrate Spain's adoption, when under Roman domination, of the invader's techniques – bronze law tablets, sculptures, mosaics (including the 3C Labours of Hercules), sarcophagi, ceramics and, in particular, a hydraulic pump made of bronze – and later how she developed a Hispanic palaeo-Christian art which incorporated ideas from Byzantium.

Medieval and Renaissance Decorative Art* – *Galleries 27-35*. In this section are the magnificent votive crowns of Guarrazar** dating from the Visigoth period. Most of them were offered by the 7C Visigoth King Recceswinth and are made of embossed gold plaques decorated with pearls, revealing a mixture of Germanic and Byzantine techniques.

This section is also devoted to the incomparable art of Muslim Spain. Among other objects, ivory caskets are displayed. Gallery 31 shows the Romanesque portal from the Monasterio de San Pedro de Arlanza (12C) and contains some of the treasures from San Isidoro de León, in particular the magnificent 11C ivory processional cross**. Rooms 32 and 33 display various exhibits of Romanesque and Gothic art, including engravings, grilles and capitals. The 14C polychrome wooden chairs from the Monasterio de las Clarisas de Astudillo (Palencia) are particularly worthy of note. Romanesque tombs and capitals, together

Martín Márquez/MICHELIN   **Museo Arqueológico Nacional**

with Gothic sculpture in subsequent galleries, continue to show deep Moorish influence. *Gallery 35* is the reconstruction of a Mudéjar home, with furnishings including carved desks.

Art des 16ᵉ et 19ᵉ s. – *Galleries 37 and 38.* In the 17C, and with even more fervour in the 18-19C, under the Bourbons, the building of many royal palaces developed the decorative arts trade. These included porcelain from the Buen Retiro and Talavera workshops, and crystal made in Royal manufactories.

North of the Museo Arqueológico are the Jardines del Descubrimiento (Discovery Gardens), an extension to plaza de Colón with massive carved stone blocks, monuments to the discovery of the New World. Madrid's Centro Cultural is below street level, beneath Plaza de Colón.

Museo Lázaro Galdiano★★

☏ 91 561 60 84. The museum in the neo-Classical mansion is bequest to the nation by José Lázaro Galdiano (1863-1947), a great art lover, and home to his invaluable **collections★★**. The ground floor traces the evolution of the artist and displays a collection of objects and paintings from various periods. There are good examples of

J. Martín Márquez/MICHELIN

Spanish painting (*Lazarus and his Sisters* by the Master of Perea; *Portrait of Charles III* by Mengs; *San Diego de Alcalá* by **Zurbarán**; *Anne of Austria* by Sánchez Coello). The "treasure room" holds outstanding gold and silver work and precious gems. There are other European paintings on this floor as well (*Christ Bound to the Column* by Naccherino; *Lady Sondes* by Reynolds).

On the 1st floor, the rooms are full of precious furniture and the ceilings covered in frescoes. The works on this floor are all Spanish, from the 15-18C. They incluye magnificent Gothic and Renaissance paintings, paintings by Zurbarán, El Greco, Carreño de Miranda, Claudio Coello, *a child's head* attributed to Velázquez and a small room with several Goyas, including *The Witches' Sabbath.*

The second floor is devoted to European art. Of particular interest are the works from the Flemish School (**Hieronymus Bosch**, Benson, Metsys, Brueghel the Younger, etc.); there are also noteworthy Italian, German, Dutch, French and English works.

On the 3rd floor you will find most of the decorative arts collection (more than 4,000 items): **ivory and enamels*****, ceramics, fabrics, fans, weapons, etc.

Esfinge alada, Museo Arqueológico

Museo del Ejército*
(Army Museum)
☏ 91 522 89 77.

A wide range of weapons and equipment (some 27 000 objects) are displayed in the vast rooms of the Palacio del Buen Retiro which was built in 1631. Arms and armour (16C), flags, banners, trophies, paintings and sculptures trace Spain's military history.

Museo Nacional de Artes Decorativas
(Decorative Arts Museum)
☏ 91 532 64 99.

This museum is housed in a small 19C palace. It contains a splendid collection of furniture and objects (porcelain, chandeliers, clocks, rugs, etc.). The displays range from 15C Mudéjar rugs to Castilian carved desks and Modernist furniture from Europe (1880/1940) as well as a beautiful 18C crèche in the Neapolitan style. Several rooms serve to re-create interiors such as a chapel with a Mudéjar ceiling and walls covered with **"guardamecíes"** (painted leather), and a 17C Valencian kitchen, completely covered in tiles.

Museo Naval
☏ 91 379 52 99.

The rooms display ship **models***, books, nautical instruments, weapons, portraits, navigation charts and paintings of naval battles. Of particular interest is the **map of Juan de la Cosa****, an invaluable document drawn in 1500, on which the American continent appears for the very first time.

Museo de Cera
(Waxworks Museum)
☐ ☏ 91 319 46 81.

This museum contains wax figures from Spanish history and contemporary celebrities in a realistic setting.

MUSEO DEL EJERCITO

Façade of the Museo del Ejército

Centro

Real Academia de Bellas Artes de San Fernando*
(San Fernando Royal Fine Arts Academy)

☎ 91 524 08 64. Founded in 1752, during the reign of Ferdinand VI, the picture gallery has a valuable collection of 16C-20C European paintings. Of particular interest are the Spanish paintings from the Golden Age, superbly represented with works by José Ribera, Zurbarán, Murillo, Alonso Cano (Christ Crucified) and Velázquez. The 18C is also present with works by artists with Bourbon connections (Van Loo, Mengs, Giaquinto, Tiepolo and Bayeu). The works in the room devoted to Goya, the most important in the museum, with his Self-portrait and a series of studio paintings (The Asylum, Inquisition Scene) are from the same century. Worthy of note in the collection of European paintings are the enigmatic Spring by Arcimboldo and the Descent by Martín de Vos. There are also 20C works by artists such as **Picasso**, Juan Gris, Chillida and Tàpies.

Museo Municipal
(Municipal Museum)

☎ 91 588 86 74. This interesting museum is housed in the former city hospice, an 18C building with a superb **portal**** built by Pedro de Ribera in Churrigueresque style. The different sections of the museum retrace the history of the city from its origins to the present day, with particular emphasis on the periods under the Habsburgs and Bourbons. Its wide-ranging collections (paintings, ceramics, furniture, coins etc) included porcelain from the Buen Retiro factory and an **1830 model of Madrid***, by Gil de Palacio.

Museo Romántico

☎ 91 448 10 71 (closed for restoration). This museum paints an accurate picture of life in the 19th century. Its exhibits include a somewhat disorganised collection of paintings, miscellaneous objects and furniture.

J. Malburet/MICHELIN

Corrida Poster

Other district

San Antonio de la Florida★

☎ 91 542 07 22. The chapel, built in 1798 under Charles IV, and painted by Goya, contains the remains of the famous artist. The frescoes★★ on the cupola illustrate a religious theme, the miracle of St Anthony of Padua – but the crowd witnessing the miracle is of a far more worldly nature, as Goya used the beautiful women of 18C Madrid as models. The result is a marvellous portrait of Madrid society at the time.

Plaza Monumental de las Ventas★ (Bullring)

The bullring (1931), known as the cathedral of bullfighting, is Spain's largest, with a seating capacity of 22 300. Adjoining it is a **Museo Taurino** (Bullfighting Museum) (☎ 91 725 18 57) in honour of the great bullfighters.

Museo Sorolla★

☎ 91 310 15 84. This eclectic 19C museum e is in the Madrid home of **Joaquín Sorolla** (1863-1923). Born in Valencia, this painter remains famous for his beach scenes and his work with colour and light. On the ground floor, several rooms are open to the public, including the artist's workshop. The rooms on the upper floor display works including: *The Mother* (1895), *El balandrito* (1909), *La Bata rosa* (1916), *La Sieste* (1911).

Museo de... (City Museum)

☎ 91 588 65 99. A stroll through the museum's rooms (third and fourth floors) provides the visitor with a journey through the history of Madrid, from prehistory through to the present day. Special mention should be made of the superb **models★** of various parts of the city and of some of the city's most emblematic buildings.

Museo del Ferrocarril (Railway Museum)

☎. ☎ 902 22 88 22. Installed in the Delicias station, the oldest in Madrid. This wrought-iron and glass station, built in 1880, has a collection of steam engines, a restaurant car in which visitors can still enjoy a cup of coffee, electric locomotives etc. It is an ideal museum for children, who will have an opportunity to climb inside some of the exhibits.

Museo Nacional de Ciencia y Tecnología (National Science and Technology Museum)

☎ 91 530 31 21. The museum has put on show just a small percentage of its extraordinary collection of scientific objects. In one room, where a view of the sky has been reproduced, the museum has set out instruments used for navigation and astronomy. These include a cross-staff★★ and a 16C astrolabe by the Flemish astronomer Arsenius.

Faunia

7km/4.5mi from Madrid along the A 3. Once past the M 40, turn off to Valdebernardo.
☺ ☎ *91 301 62 10.*

This extensive leisure park covering 140 000m²/167 300sq yd re-creates different ecosystems existing on the planet. A 4.5km/3mi journey through the park enables visitors to discover some 4 500 small- and medium-sized animals and over 70 000 trees and plants. The pavilions, half-buried in the earth, are dedicated to specific subjects: tropical jungles, Mediterranean forests, the north and south poles, pollination and insects, the world at night, the underground world, animal food resources, and

Dolphins, Faunia

© TURESPAÑ

biodiversity. The park also has a good selection of shops and restaurants.

El Pardo

17km/10.5mi NW. The town, now on the outskirts of Madrid, has grown around one of the royal residences. Its surrounding forests of holm oak were once the traditional hunting preserve of Spanish monarchs.

Palacio Real* – ☎ *91 376 15 00.*

The royal palace was built by Philip III (1598-1621) on the site of Philip II's (1556-98) palace which had been destroyed in a fire in 1604, and remodelled by Sabatini in 1772. Franco lived here for 35 years; today, it is used by foreign Heads of State on official visits.

As you walk through the reception rooms and private apartments you will see elegant ensembles from Charles IV's collections including furniture, chandeliers and clocks. More than **200 tapestries*** hang on the walls; the majority are 18C from the Real Fábrica de Tápices (Royal Tapestry Factory) in Madrid based on cartoons by Goya, Bayeu, González Ruiz and Van Loo. The Renaissance frescoes of **Gaspar Becerra**, disciple of Michelangelo, in the 16C Queen's Tower, have recently been added to this beautiful collection.

Casita del Príncipe (The Prince's Pavilion) – ☎ *91 376 03 29.*

The pavilion, built in 1772 for the children of the future Charles IV and his wife María Luisa, was completely remodelled by Juan de Villanueva in 1784. It is a single-storey building of brick and stone decorated in the extremely ornate, refined taste fashionable in the late 18C with silk hangings and Pompeian style ceilings.

La Quinta – ☎ *91 376 03 29 / 15 00.* The former residence of the Duke of Arco became Crown property in 1745. Inside, elegant early-19C wallpaper embellishes the walls.

Convento de Capuchinos (Capuchin Monastery) – ☎ *91 376 08 00.*

A chapel contains one of the major works of Spanish sculpture, a polychrome wood figure of **Christ Recumbent*** by Gregorio Fernández, commissioned by Philip III in 1605.

Warner Bros Park*

30km/18mi S of Madrid via the A 4. Follow the signs. ⌚ *Check opening hours. 1-day ticket: 32€ (child: 24€), 2-day ticket: 48€ (child: 36€).* ☎ *918 211 234.*

This theme park carries you away into the fabulous world of Warner Brothers. Divided in five different zones, the park has rides, attractions, bars, restaurants and shops.

Hollywood Boulevard – This section of the park concentrates on the glamour of the most famous streets in Hollywood.

© TURESPAÑA

Movie WB World Studios – True to the Warner Brothers image, the studio produces live car chases, gunfire, explosions and other spectacular stunts. Don't miss the "Haunted Hotel", with its hair-raising special effects, or the "Police Academy" and "Lethal Weapon" shows.

Super Heroes World – This is part of the park is ruled by famous characters from the comic book world. Live exciting adventures in Metropolis with Superman or in the shadowy city of Gotham where Batman struggles against evil forces.

The rides include super rollercoasters called "The Man of Steel" and "The Flight of Batman". If you go for the really

Cartoon Village

wild ones, try "The Enigma's Vengeance" – a free fall of 100 metres!

The Old West Territory – Let the cowboy inside you roam the Wild West. Test your courage on the wooden wagons of the "Wild Wild West" rollercoaster or take a plunge down white water rapids. Don't leave without exploring the Rio Bravo and the gold mine.

Cartoon Village – Young children will enjoy this marvellous village where cartoon characters greet them: Daffy Duck, Tweety Pie, Bugs Bunny, Tom and Jerry. The main attractions here are the Tom et Jerry rollercoaster and the visit of the ACME studios (water games).

Excursions

Alcalá de Henares ★

Population: 162 780. Michelin maps 575 and 576 K 19–32km/ 20mi W via A 2. 🚹 Pl. de los Santos Niños, ☎ 91 881 06 34.

In 1998, the university and historic centre of Alcalá were declared a World Heritage site by UNESCO. It is a pleasant town with a **historic centre★** adorned with 16C-17C buildings — predominantly old colleges and convents — and attractive, spacious squares.

Antigua Universidad or Colegio de San Ildefonso★

☎ 91 885 40 00. The old university building, now used to house the university education offices, stands on the plaza de San Diego. Its beautiful **Plateresque façade★** (1543) is by Rodrigo Gil de Hontañón and comprises three sections crowned with a balustrade. On the central section, framed by the cordon of the Franciscans note the large imperial escutcheon of Charles V decorating the pediment. The majestic 17C **Patio Mayor** was designed by Juan Gómez de Mora, architect of the Plaza Mayor and Ayuntamiento (Town Hall) in Madrid; at the centre is a well-head with a swan motif, the emblem of Cardinal Cisneros. Across the Patio de los Filósofos, stands the delightful **Patio Trilingüe** (1557) where Latin, Greek and Hebrew were taught. This 16C Renaissance patio, a model of simplicity, belonged to the Colegio de San Jerónimo. The **Paraninfo★** (1520), a small room used for the awarding of the Cervantes literary prize. The decoration includes a gallery delicately embellished in the Plateresque style, with superb Mudéjar **artesonado★★** work, comprising six-pointed star ornamentation.

Capilla de San Ildefonso★ – *Next to the university.* This fine early-16C chapel was built for use as the university's church. Its single nave and the presbytery are both crowned with magnificent **Mudéjar artesonado** ceilings. The delicate **stucco** decoration shows the stylistic

CERVANTES

CERVANTES

Adventure and storytelling are the words that best sum up the life of **Miguel de Cervantes Saavedra** (1547-1616). As a young man he spent four years in Italy after which he enlisted and fought at the Battle of Lepanto (1571) where he was wounded. In 1575 he was captured by the Turks, taken off to Algeria as a slave and rescued after five years by the Fathers of the Holy Trinity. In 1605 he published the first part of *Don Quixote* which was an immense and immediate success. In this tragicomic masterpiece an elderly gentleman sets out as a doughty knight errant in search of adventure, hoping to redress wrongs in the terms of the storybooks he loves; he is accompanied by his simple but astute squire, Sancho Panza. The interaction of the ideal and the real, the true and the illusory, reveals the meditations of a man of 58 deeply involved in philosophy, life and the Spain of his day.

EXCURSIONS

URESPAÑA

Façade of the University

evolution of this technique from the late-Gothic period to the Plateresque style. The presbytery houses the **mausoleum**** of Cardinal Cisneros, a work by Domenico Fancelli and Bartolomé Ordóñez. Carved in Carrara marble, it is one of the finest examples of 16C Spanish sculpture.

Catedral Magistral

Plaza de los Santos Niños. Although the cathedral was built between 1497 and 1515, it has since been remodelled on several occasions. On the exterior, note the central portal, with its mix of Gothic, Plateresque and Mudéjar features. The late-Gothic interior contains some attractive wrought-iron **grilles**. The cloisters (*entrance on calle Tercia*) house the **Museo de la Catedral** (☎ *91 888 09 30*).

Palacio Arzobispal

Plaza de Palacio. In the 13C, the bishops of Toledo, the lords of Alcalá, erected a sizeable palace-fortress on this site. The present-day Renaissance **façade**, designed by Alonso de Covarrubias, originally fronted the courtyard of the palace. The large Baroque coat of arms was added at a later date.

The adjoining plaza de San Bernardo is lined by the **Convento de San Bernardo**, whose 17C church is crowned by an impressive elliptical dome, and the **Museo Arqueológico de la Comunidad de Madrid**. (☎ *91 879 66 66*).

81

$\mathcal{A}$ranjuez★★

EXCURSIONES

*Population: 35 872. Michelin maps 575 and 576 L 19 – 47km/29mi S via A 4. You can also travel on the **Tren de la Fresa**, a small steam train, a copy of the train that was put into service for the first time in 1851; The trip includes a guided tour of the Palacio and the museums (weekends and holidays from Apr-Oct ☎ 902 22 88 22).*
🚩 Pl. de San Antonio 9.
☎ 91 891 04 27.

$\mathcal{A}$ranjuez, on the banks of the Tagus (Tajo), appears like an oasis at the centre of the harsh Castilian plain. The town is renowned for its greenery and leafy avenues, particularly around the royal palace.

The shaded walks described by writers, sung by composers (Joaquín Rodrigo's famous Concierto de Aranjuez) and painted by artists (the Catalan, Rusiñol) are now popular

THE ARANJUEZ REVOLT
(EL MOTÍN DE ARANJUEZ)

In March 1808, Charles IV, his queen and the prime minister, Godoy, were at Aranjuez. They were preparing to flee (on 18 March) first to Andalucía, then to America, as Godoy had allowed Napoleon's armies free passage to Portugal through Spain the year before. In Portugal, the French were fighting the Portuguese who were strongly supported by the British. The Spanish people, however, had objected to the passage of the French and Godoy had advised his king to follow the Portuguese royal house (which had fled from Lisbon to Brazil) into exile.

On the night of 17 March, Godoy's mansion was attacked by followers of the heir apparent, Prince Ferdinand; Charles IV dismissed his minister and was compelled to abdicate in favour of his son. This was not enough, however: Napoleon summoned both to Bayonne and made them abdicate in his own favour (5 May).

These intrigues and the presence of a French garrison in Madrid stirred the Spaniards to the revolt of May 1808 which marked the beginning of the War of Independence.

The magnificent **Revolt Fair** is held every year during the first week of September. A hundred participants recreate scenes of the main events of the revolt.

© TURESPAÑA.

with Madrileños, especially at weekends.

ROYAL PALACE AND GARDENS★★

The Catholic Monarchs enjoyed staying in the original 14C palace, then Emperor Charles V enlarged the domain, but the present palace is mainly the result of an initiative by Philip II who called on the future architects of the Escorial to erect a new palace surrounded by gardens.

In the 18C, the town became one of the principal royal residences and was considerably embellished under the Bourbons.

Palacio Real★

☎ 91 892 15 32. This Classical-style royal palace of brick and stone was built in the 16C and restored in the 18C. In spite of many modifications it retains considerable unity of style and symmetry. The court of honour, overlooking a vast outer square, is framed by the main building with wings at right angles on either side; domed pavilions mark the angles.

Palacio Real

The apartments have been left as they were at the end of the 19C.

The grand staircase was designed by the Italian Giacomo Bonavia during the reign of Philip V. The bust of Louis XIV by Coysevox recalls Philip V's French ancestry. In María Luisa's apartments, in an antechamber, are paintings by the Neapolitan artist Luca Giordano, and in the music room, a piano presented by Eugenia de Montijo to Isabel II.

The **Salón del Trono** (Throne Room), with crimson velvet hangings and Rococo furnishings, has a ceiling painted with an allegory of monarchy – ironically it was in this room that Charles IV signed his abdication after the attack on 17 March 1808.

The **Salón de Porcelana**★★ (Porcelain Room) is the palace's most appealing and gracefully appointed room. It is covered in white garlanded porcelain tiles, illustrating in coloured high relief scenes of Chinese life, exotica and children's games, all made in the Buen Retiro factory in Madrid in 1763.

In the king's apartments a music room precedes the Smoking or Arabian Room – a diverting reproduction of the Hall of the Two Sisters in the Alhambra in Granada. A fine Mengs *Crucifixion* hangs in the bedroom, and the walls of another room are decorated with **203 small pictures** painted on rice paper with Oriental-style motifs. At the end of the guided tour you can also visit a museum of palace life at the time of Alfonso XIII, where you will see rooms and exhibits which include a gymnasium and a tricycle.

Parterre and Jardín de la Isla★ (Parterre and Island Garden)

☎ 91 542 00 59. The **Parterre** extending along the palace's east front is a formal garden laid out by the Frenchman Boutelou in 1746.

The **Jardín de la Isla** was laid out on an artificial island in the Tajo river in the 16C. Cross the canal which once drove mill wheels to reach the park and its many fountains hidden among copses of chestnut, ash and poplar trees and banks and hedges of boxwood.

Jardín del Príncipe★★ (The Prince's Garden)

Entrance in calle de la Rein.
☎ 91 542 00 59. The garden beside the Tajo is more a vast gracefully laid-out park (150ha/ 371 acres). It has grilles and four monumental gateways by Juan de Villanueva.

In 1763, called upon by the future Charles IV, Boutelou landscaped the park according to the romantic vision of nature fashionable at the end of the 18C.

Casa del Labrador★★ (The Labourer's Cottage) – ☎ 91 891 03 05.

The cottage, named after the peasant farm which originally stood on the site, stands at the eastern end of the Jardín del Príncipe and is a Versailles type Trianon built on the whim of Charles IV in a neo-Classical style similar to that of the Royal Palace but with more luxurious decoration.

The interior, a reflection of Spanish Bourbon taste, is an excellent example of sumptuous 18C decoration: Pompeian style ceilings, embroidered silk hangings, mahogany doors, marble floors, furniture and lamps, canvases by Bambrilla, clocks and porcelain.

The statue gallery is embellished with Greek busts and a marble floor covering inlaid with Roman mosaics from Mérida. The French clock in the middle of the gallery incorporates a reproduction of Trajan's column. The María Luisa room has remarkable embroidered hangings made up of 97 small pictures show-ing a variety of views. In the centre of the ballroom stand a magnificent malachite table and chair given to Charles IV by the Tsar Alexander III. The Platinum Room, or Gabinete de Platino, is decorated with gold, platinum and bronze inlays while the figure of a bird in the anteroom is carved from a single piece of ivory.

Casa de Marinos (The Sailors' House) – ☏ *91 891 03 05*. A museum beside the former landing stage contains the **falúas reales**** *(royal vessels)* which once made up the Tajo fleet of launches that ferried the royal family and guests to the Labourer's Cottage.

Gardens in autumn

Monasterio de El Escorial★★★

Michelin maps 575 or 576 K 17. 49km/29mi. NW of Madrid via the A6 and the M 505. There is a good **view★** of the monastery and the surrounding countryside from **Silla de Felipe II** (Philip II's Seat), from where the king oversaw its construction *(turn left beyond the monastery into the road marked Entrada Herrería-Golf and follow signs to the Silla de Felipe II).* ⬛ *Grimaldi 2, 28200 San Lorenzo de El Escorial, ☎ 91 890 53 13.*

The impressive monastery of San Lorenzo el Real, or El Escorial, stands at the foot of Monte Abantos on the southern slopes of the Sierra de Guadarrama at an altitude of 1 065m/3 494ft. This symbolic building, commissioned by King **Philip II** and designed by Juan de Herrera, heralded the creation of a style that combined the grandeur of a great palace with the austerity of a committed monastery.

Visiting the Monastery
Allow half a day. ☎ *91 890 78 18.*
It is said that the monastery recalls St Lawrence's martyrdom with its gridiron ground plan. It measures 206m x 161m (676ft x 528ft) and is built of grey granite – the austerity of the stone serving to emphasise, if anything, the severity of the architecture. Only the four towers, one on each corner, break up the long horizontal perspective.
Palacios★★ (Royal Apartments) – The northeast section of the building is occupied by the Bourbon palace; Philip II lived in the section around the apse of the church and the cloisters.
A staircase built in the time of Charles IV goes up *(3rd floor)* to the **Palacio de los Borbones** (Bourbon Apartments). These are sumptuous with Pompeian ceilings and fine **tapestries★**.
The style of decoration changes, introducing the austerity of the Habsburgs. The large **Sala de las Batallas** (Battle Gallery) contains frescoes (1587): on the south wall, of the Victory at Higueruela in the 15C against the Moors and on the north wall, the Victory at St-Quentin against the French.

IN MEMORY OF SAN LORENZO
On 10 August 1557, St Lawrence's Day, **Philip II's** forces defeated the French at the memorable battle of St-Quentin. In commemoration the king decided to build a monastery and dedicate it to the saint. It was consigned to the Hieronymites and served as the royal palace and pantheon.
The project was stupendous and was completed in a mere 21 years (1563-84) which is why the building has an exceptional unity of style.
The general designs of the first architect, Juan de Toledo, were followed, after his death in 1567 by his assistant **Juan de Herrera**, who, however, is responsible for the final overall elegance. Reaction to the sumptuous ornamentation fashionable in Charles V's reign spurred the architects to produce a sober monument with clean cut, majestic lines.

TURESPAÑA

Monasterio de El Escorial

The restraint of the **habitaciones de Felipe II** (Philip II's apartments) *(2nd floor)* is all the more striking after the luxury of the Bourbon rooms. Those of the Infanta Isabel Clara Eugenia, like those of her father, comprise a suite of relatively small rooms in which the principal decoration derives from dados of Talavera ceramic tiles. The king's bedroom, where he died in 1598, aged 71, is directly off the church. A communicating door allowed him to be present during services and contemplate the high altar from his bed. The paintings in the apartments include a *St Christopher* by Patinir and a portrait of the king in his old age by Pantoja de la Cruz. Facing the gardens and the plain, the Salón del Trono (Throne Room) and the Sala de los Retratos (Portrait Gallery). Finally, visitors are shown Philip's sedan chair in which he was carried when no longer able to walk.

Panteones** (Pantheons) – Access is through the Patio de los Evangelistas (Evangelists' Courtyard) in which the walls are painted with frescoes by Tibaldi (east wall) and his followers.

A marble and jasper staircase leads down to the **Panteón de los Reyes***** (Royal Pantheon) which lies beneath the chancel. It contains the mortal remains of all the Spanish monarchs from the time of Emperor Charles V, with the exception of Philip V, Ferdinand VI and Amadeus of Savoy.

The chapel, which is octagonal in shape, was begun in the reign of Philip III and completed in 1654. The main architect was Juan Bautista Crescenci. Facing the door is the jasper altar; on either side stand the 26 marble and bronze sarcophagi in wall niches. The kings are on the left and the queens whose sons succeeded to the throne, on the right.

The 19C **Panteón de los Infantes*** (Infantes' Pantheon) includes not only royal children but also queens whose children did not succeed to the throne. The decoration includes delicately carved sculptures. Climatic conditions are such that the room has been well preserved.

Salas Capitulares* (Chapter houses) – Two fine rooms, with ceilings painted by Italian artists with grotesques and frescoes, form a museum of Spanish (16C and 17C) and Italian (16C) religious painting.

The first room contains canvases by El Greco and Ribera, a *St Jerome* by Titian, and *Joseph's Tunic* painted by Velázquez in Rome.

The second room has works from the 16C Venetian School, including paintings by Tintoretto, Veronese and Titian (Ecce Homo).

A room at the back contains works by Bosch and his followers: the *Haywain* and the *Crown of Thorns*.

Basílica**

Herrera based his final plan for the basilica on Italian drawings,

Chapter house, Monasterio de El Escori

introducing an architectural novelty, a **flat vault**, in the atrium. The church's interior owes much to St Peter's in Rome with a Greek cross plan, a 92m/302ft high cupola above the transept crossing supported by four colossal pillars, and barrel vaulting in the transept. The frescoes in the nave vaulting were painted by Luca Giordano in Charles II's reign. Wide, red marble steps lead to the sanctuary which has paintings on the vaulting of the lives of Christ and the Virgin by Cambiasso. The massive **retable**, designed by Herrera, is 30m/100ft tall and is composed of four registers of jasper, onyx and red marble columns between which stand 15 bronze sculptures by Leone and Pompeo Leoni. The tabernacle is also by Herrera. On opposite sides of the chancel lie the tombs of Charles V and Philip II: the sculptor Pompeo Leoni showed them praying with their families.

The door at the end on the right is the one communicating with Philip II's room.

In the first chapel off the north aisle is the *Martyrdom of St Maurice* by Rómulo Cincinato, which Philip II preferred to that of El Greco (*see below*). In the adjoining chapel is a magnificent sculpture of Christ carved by Benvenuto Cellini in 1562.

Patio de los Reyes (Kings' Courtyard) – One of the three Classical gateways in the palace's principal façade opens onto this courtyard. The court is named after the statues of the kings of Judea which adorn the majestic west front of the church.

Biblioteca★★ (Library) – *2nd floor*. The gallery is 54m/177ft

long and richly decorated; the shelving, designed by Herrera, is of exotic woods; the ceiling, sumptuously painted by Tibaldi; the magnificent portraits of Charles V, Philip II and Philip III by Pantoja de la Cruz, and one of Charles II by Carreño.

Philip II furnished the library with over 10 000 books of which many suffered in the 1671 fire and from the ravages of Napoleon's army. It is now a public library with over 40 000 books and some 2 700 manuscripts dating from the 5C to the 18C. The unusual presentation of the books on the shelves, with the spine facing inwards, is for preservation purposes.

In the cases, on the marble tables, are precious manuscripts. **Nuevos Museos**★★ (New Museums) – The **Museo de Pintura** (Picture Museum) contains an interesting collection of works illustrating religious themes.

Works by Titian, Veronese (*Annunciation*), Tintoretto (*Nativity*), Van Dyck, Van der Weyden (*Calvary*), and Ribera (*St Jerome Penitent, the Philosopher Chrysippus* and *Aesop*) are on exhibit. alongside works by Zurbarán (*St Peter of Alcántara* and the *Presentation of the Virgin*), Alonso Cano and Luca Giordano. There is one small Rubens.

In the vaulted cellars, the **Architecture Museum** has displays about the construction of the monestery: the artisans who built it, the cost of the work, drawing by Herrera, etc. On the ground floor, the painting section gives a place of honour to **Greco's** work, *The Martyrdom of St Maurice and his Legions*★.

J. Malburet/MICHELIN

Other royal buildings
Casita del Príncipe* (Prince's or Lower Pavilion) – *SE along the road to the station.* ☎ *91 890 59 02/3.*

Charles III commissioned Juan de Villanueva to build a leisure lodge for the future Charles IV in the Prince's Gardens. Its exquisite decoration makes it a jewel of a palace, in miniature. There are painted **Pompeian*** style ceilings by Maella and Vicente Gómez, silk hangings, canvases by Luca Giordano, chandeliers, porcelain and a beautiful mahogany and marble dining room.
Casita del Infante (Infante's or Upper Pavilion) – *3km/2mi SW beyond the golf course.* ☎ *91 890 59 03.*

This lodge was designed by Villanueva for the Infante Gabriel, Charles IV's younger brother. The interior is furnished in the style of the period; the first floor was arranged as apartments for Prince Juan Carlos before his accession to the throne.

Valle de los Caídos**
16km/10mi NW on the M 600 and the M 527. ☎ *91 890 56 11.* In the heart of the sierra de Guadarrama, the Valle de los Caídos, the Valley of the Fallen, built between 1940 and 1958, is a striking monument to the dead of the Spanish Civil War (1936-39). The road leads to the foot of the esplanade in front of the basilica, which is hollowed out of the rock face itself and is dominated by a monumental Cross.

Courtyard of the Monasterio de El Escorial

Basílica** – The basilica's west door in the austere granite façade is a bronze work crowned by a *Pietà* by Juan de Ávalos. The interior is a fine wrought-iron screen with 40 statues and a 262m/860ft nave (St Peter's, Rome: 186m/610ft; St Paul's, London: 152m/500ft) lined with six chapels [devoted to the Virgin Mary] between which have been hung eight copies of 16C Brussels tapestries of the Apocalypse. Above the crossing, a **cupola***, 42m/138ft in diameter, is sumptuously decorated with mosaic. On the altar stands a painted wood figure of Christ Crucified, set against a tree trunk; it is the work of the sculptor Beovides. At the foot of the altar is the funerary stone of José Antonio Primo de Rivera, son of the dictator and founder of the Falangist Party, and that of Franco. Ossuaries contain coffins of 40 000 soldiers and civilians from both sides in the Civil War.

La Cruz* – The Cross by the architect Diego Méndez, is 125m/410ft high (150m/492ft including the base), the width from fingertip to fingertip, 46m/150ft. The immense statues of the Evangelists around the plinth and the four cardinal virtues above are by Juan de Ávalos. There is a good **view** from the base *(access by funicular)*. The large building showing Herreran influence on the far side of the valley from the basilica is a Benedictine monastery, seminary and social studies centre.

Segovia ★★★

Michelin maps 575 to 576 J 17 – Population: 57.617. 91km/55mi NE via A 6, AP 6 and AP 61. For the best view of the site, drive along the cuesta de los Hoyos and paseo de Santo Domingo de Guzmán. ⏺ pl. Mayor 10, 40001, ☎ 921 46 03 34; pl. de Azoguejo, 1, 4001, ☎ 921 46 29 06.

This austere, imposing city, situated at an altitude of 1 000m/3 280ft, has a unique site perched on a triangular rock rising like an island out of the surrounding Castilian plain at the confluence of the River Eresma and River Clamores. Enclosed within its sturdy walls is a complicated maze of narrow streets dotted with impressive Roman monuments and noble mansions.

LA CIUDAD VIEJA★★ (OLD TOWN)
Visit: 4hr – Follow the itinerary on the plan

Acueducto romano★★★
This aqueduct is one of the finest examples of Roman engineering still standing today.

The simple, elegant structure was built during the reign of Trajan in the 1C to bring water from the River Acebeda in the Sierra de Fuenfría to the upper part of the town. It is 728m/2 388ft long, rises to a maximum height of 28m/92ft in plaza del Azoguejo where the ground is lowest, and consists throughout of two tiers of arches.

Casa de los Picos
The house, faced closely with diamond pointed stones, is the most original of Segovia's 15C mansions.

Casa del Conde de Alpuente
The elegant façade of this 15C Gothic house is adorned with *esgrafiado* designs.

Alhóndiga
This 15C granary has been transformed into an exhibition room.

Plaza de San Martín★
The square is the most evocative of historic Segovia. It is

THE "COMUNEROS"

In 1520, just three years after he had landed in the Asturian port of Tazones to take possession of the crowns of Castilla and Aragón, the Habsburg Charles I was forced to abandon his new kingdom in order to be proclaimed Holy Roman Emperor (as Charles V). The same year, an uprising started in the towns and cities of Castilla that was to become known as the revolt of the Comunidades (town forces). The catalysts of the uprising included the aforementioned abandonment of his kingdom, Charles V's eagerness to surround himself with a Flemish court and his attempt to impose new taxes to pay for the pomp and splendour of his new empire. At the root of the Comuneros movement was the opposition of Castilian towns, the middle classes and merchants to the alliance established between Charles V and the landowning aristocracy. Numerous town forces, under the leadership of Juan de Padilla in Toledo, Francisco Maldonado in Salamanca and Juan Bravo in Segovia, rose up against royal authority, but were finally crushed at Villalar in 1521.

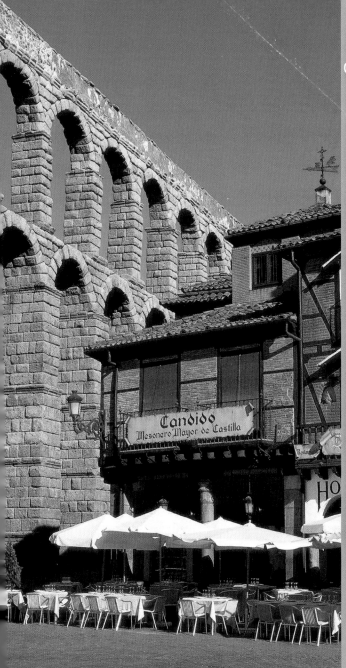

Candido
Mesonero Mayor de Castilla

ESGRAFIADOS

Geometric designs, or *esgrafiados*, are one of the most characteristic features of Segovian architecture. The word derives from the Italian *graffiare*, meaning "to scratch". The technique consists of scratching – following a pre-existing design – an outer layer, to expose an underlying layer of a different colour tone.

formed of two small squares joined by a flight of steps. The statue is of Juan Bravo. Around the square stand the **Casa del Siglo XV** (15C House) with a gallery beneath the eaves, the 16C tower of the **Casa de los Lozoya**, the Plateresque façade of the **Casa de Solier** (Solier Mansion, also known as Casa de Correas) and the ornate entrances to big houses. In the middle of the square is the 12C **Iglesia de San Martín★**, a church framed on three sides by a covered gallery on pillars with carved strapwork and animal figures on the capitals.

Museo Esteban Vicente. ☎ 921 46 37 38. The museum is housed in the palace of Henry IV in the so-called Hospital de Viejos (Old People's Hospital). The only trace of the original building is the fine chapel with a Mudéjar ceiling which has been converted into an auditorium. The museum was created following a donation by the artist Esteban Vicente (1903-2001), the only Spanish member of the New York School, and exhibits his work from 1925 to 1997.

The 17C **antigua cárcel** (Old Prison) has a decorative Baroque pediment.

Plaza Mayor

Dominated by the impressive cathedral, the arcaded square with its terrace cafés is a popular meeting-place with Segovians. Among the buildings surrounding the square are the Ayuntamiento (town hall) and the Teatro Juan Bravo.

Catedral★★

☎ 921 46 22 05. This was built during the reign of Emperor Charles V to replace the cathedral that had been destroyed during the Comuneros' Revolt in 1521. It is an example of the survival of the Gothic style in the 16C when Renaissance architecture was at its height. The beautiful golden stone, the stepped east end with pinnacles and delicate balustrades and the tall tower, bring considerable grace to the massive building. Among the chapels, which are closed by fine wrought-iron screens, the first off the south aisle contains as altarpiece an *Entombment* by Juan de Juni. The *coro* stalls, in the late-15C Flamboyant Gothic style, are from the earlier cathedral.

Claustro★ – The 15C cloisters from the former cathedral, which stood near the Alcázar, were transported stone by stone and rebuilt on the new site. The Sala Capitular (chapter house) has beautiful 17C Brussels **tapestries★**.

Alcázar★★

☎ 921 46 07 59. The Alcázar, standing on a cliff overlooking the valley, was built above a former fortress in the early 13C and modified in the 15C and 16C by Henry IV and

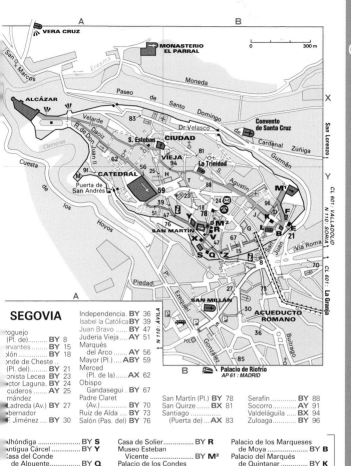

SEGOVIA

Philip II respectively. In 1764, Charles III converted the building into a **Real Colegio de Artillería** (Royal Artillery School), but in 1862 it suffered a devastating fire which spared the academy's library and very little else. Reconstruction was completed at the end of the 19C, during the reign of Alfonso XII, hence its neo-Gothic appearance today. The furniture and richly decorated Mudéjar *artesonado* work, mostly dating from the 15C, are original and were brought from various Castilian towns. Its keep is flanked by corbelled turrets. The main rooms of note are the Chamber Royal (Cámara Real) and the Sala de los Reyes (Monarchs' Room). The Sala del Cordón and terrace command a fine **panorama** of the fertile

J. Malburet/MICHELIN

Cathe

Eresma Valley, the Monasterio de El Parral, the Capilla de la Vera Cruz and the *meseta* beyond.

Iglesia de San Esteban (St Stephen's Church)

One of the latest (13C) and most beautiful of Segovia's Romanesque churches. The porticoes running along two of its sides have finely carved capitals.

The five-storey **tower★** has elegant bays and slender columns on the corners. The interior is in Renaissance style. Inside, the altar in the south transept has a 13C Gothic figure of Christ in polychrome wood.

Iglesia de la Trinidad (Holy Trinity Church)

This somewhat austere Romanesque church has a decorated apse where there is blind arcading and capitals carved with imaginary beasts and plant motifs.

Iglesia de San Juan de los Caballeros★

☎ 921 46 33 48. This is Segovia's oldest Romanesque church (11C). Its outstand-

ROMANESQUE CHURCHES

These beautiful churches of golden stone have common architectural features: well-rounded apses, frequently a tall square belfry beside the east end and a covered gallery where weavers' or merchants' guilds used to meet.

ing feature is the portico (taken from the church of San Nicolás) with its carvings of portrait heads, plant motifs and animals. The church, which was almost in ruins at the turn of the 20C, was bought by Daniel Zuloaga, who converted it into his home and workshop. Today it houses the **Museo Zuloaga**, exhibiting drawings by the artist and paintings by his nephew, Ignacio Zuloaga.

Plaza del Conde de Cheste

On the square stand the palaces of the **Marqués de Moya**, the **Marqués de Lozoya**, the **Condes de Cheste** and the **Marqués de Quintanar**.

Iglesia de San Sebastián

This small Romanesque church stands on one side of a quiet square.

OUTSIDE THE WALLS
Iglesia de San Millán★

☎ 921 46 38 01. The early-12C church stands in the middle of a large square which allows a full view of its pure, still primitive Romanesque lines and two porticoes with finely carved modillions and capitals. The apse has blind arcading and a decorative frieze which continues throughout the church. The transept has Moorish ribbed vaulting.

Monasterio de El Parral★

☎ 921 43 12 98. The monastery was founded by Henry IV in 1445 and later entrusted to the Hieronymites. The **church** has a Gothic nave with beautifully carved doors, a 16C altarpiece and the Plateresque tombs of the Marquis and Marchioness of Villena.

Capilla de la Vera-Cruz★

☎ 921 43 14 75. The unusual polygonal chapel was erected in the 13C, probably by the Templars. A circular corridor surrounds two small chambers. The Capilla del Lignum Crucis contains an ornate Flamboyant Gothic altar. There is a good **view** of Segovia.

Convento de Santa Cruz

The convent pinnacles, the decorated Isabelline **entrance** with a Calvary, a *Pietà*, and the emblems of the Catholic Monarchs, can be seen from the road.

Iglesia de San Lorenzo

The Romanesque church with its unusual brick belfry stands in a picturesque square surrounded by corbelled half-timbered houses.

EXCURSIONS
Palacio de La Granja de San Ildefonso★★

12km/7mi SE via CL 601. ☎ 921 47 00 19. The palace of La Granja is a little Versailles at an altitude of 1 192m/3 911ft at the foot of the Sierra de Guadarrama in the centre of Spain. It was built in 1731 by Philip V, grandson of Louis XIV, in pure nostalgia for the palace of his childhood.

El palacio – Galleries and chambers, faced with marble

or hung with crimson velvet, are lit, beneath painted ceilings and gilded stucco mouldings, by ornate chandeliers, made by the local royal workshops which became renowned in the 18C. A **Museo de Tapices**** (Tapestry Museum) on the first floor contains principally 16C Flemish hangings.

Philip V and his second wife, Isabel Farnese, are buried in a chapel in the collegiate church.

Gardens – Rocks were blown up and the ground levelled before the French landscape gardeners and sculptors could start work in the 145ha/358-acre park, inspired by the gardens and parkland of Versailles. The woodland vistas are more natural, however, the rides more rural, the intersections marked by less formal cascades. The **fountains**** begin at the Neptune Basin, go on to the New Cascade (Nueva Cascada) and end at the Fuente de la Fama, or Fame Fountain, which jets up a full 40m/131ft.

Real Fábrica de Cristales de La Granja (Royal Glass Factory) – ☎ *921 01 07 00.* Although the glass-works dates

J. Malburet/MICHELIN

back to the reign of Philip V, the present building was built in 1770, under Charles III. It is one of the few examples of industrial architecture in Spain and is now the headquarters of the National Glass Centre. A glass museum (Museo del Vidrio) is now housed inside the building.

Palacio de Riofrío★

Palacio – *11km/6.5mi SE via N 603.* ☎ *921 47 00 19. The palace stands at the foot of the Mujer Muerta mountain on a little hill surrounded by an oak forest where deer roam freely.*

Riofrío was planned by Isabel Farnese on the death of her husband, Philip V. Construction began in 1752 but though it was very big – it measures 84m x 84m (276ft x 276ft) – it was nothing more than a somewhat pretentious hunting lodge. This palatine construction was never completed and Isabel Farnese never lived in it.

It is built around a Classical-style grand central courtyard. A monumental staircase leads to sumptuously decorated apartments. It houses an amusing Hunting Museum.

Gardens, Palacio de La Granja

Toledo ★★★

Michelin Map 576 M 17 –
Population: 63.561. 71km/42mi
SW of Madrid via N 401. The
**site**★★★ is superb, particularly
seen from the carretera de cir-
cunvalación, a ring-road which
for a couple of miles parallels,
on the far bank, the almost
circular loop of the Tajo which
flows all the way round from the
Puente de Alcántara (Alcántara
Bridge). From the surrounding
hills, admire the view of the
cigarrales (country houses). The
terrace of the parador, set above
the carretera de circunvalación,
commands a superb view.
🖪 Puerta Bisagra, 45003, ☏ 925
22 08 43; pl. del Ayuntamiento 1,
_45001, ☏ 925 25 40 30._

EXCURSIONS

Toledo stands out dra-
matically against the often
luminously blue Castilian sky:
a golden city rising from a
granite eminence, encircled
by a steep ravine filled by the
green waters of the Tajo (Tagus). It is as spectacular as it
is rich in history, buildings and
art; every corner has a tale to
be told, every aspect reflects
a brilliant period of Spanish
history when the cultures of
east and west flourished and
fused: one is constantly aware
of this imprint of Christian,
Jewish and Moorish cultures
which, as in Granada, produc-
tively co-existed during the
Middle Ages.

CENTRE OF OLD TOLEDO ★★★

Allow 1 day – see itinerary on
town plan

There is something to see and
enjoy at every step in Toledo.
Walking along the maze of
narrow, winding lanes you
pass churches, old houses and
palaces.
Ringing the square before
the cathedral are the 18C
Palacio Arzobispal (Arch-
bishop's Palace), the 17C

FROM A ROMAN TOWN TO A HOLY ROMAN CITY

The Romans, appreciating the site's strategic and geographic advantage at the centre of the
peninsula, fortified and built up the settlement into a town they named Toletum. It passed, in
due course, into the hands of the barbarians, and in the 6C to the Visigoths who ultimately
made it a monarchal seat. The Visigoths, defeated at Guadelete in 711, abandoned the town
to the Moors who incorporated it in the Córdoba Emirate, until the successful revolt of the
Taifas in 1012 raised it to the position of capital of an independent kingdom. In 1085 Toledo
was conquered by Alfonso VI de León. Two years later, the king moved his capital there
from León. It is to Alfonso VII, crowned emperor there, that Toledo owes its title of imperial
city. Toledo, with its mixed Moorish, Jewish and Christian communities, began to prosper
richly. The Catholic Monarchs gave it the Monastery of St John but lost interest in the city
when they began to compare it with Granada, reconquered under their own aegis in 1492.
Emperor Charles V had the Alcázar rebuilt. Also during his reign the city took part in the
Comuneros' Revolt led by **Juan de Padilla**, a Toledan.
Progress was halted in 1561 when Philip II named Madrid as Spain's capital, leaving Toledo
as the spiritual centre, and the seat of the primacy. The events of 1936 within and without
the Alcázar, brought it briefly into the limelight of history.

Ayuntamiento (Town Hall) with its classical façade and the 14C **Audiencia** (Law Courts).

Catedral***

☎ 925 22 22 41. The cathedral is in the heart of Toledo's old quarter. Construction began in the reign of Ferdinand III (St Ferdinand) in 1227. Unlike other churches in the vicinity, the design was French Gothic but as building continued until the end of the 15C, plans were modified and the completed edifice presents a conspectus of Spanish Gothic. The church remains of outstanding interest for its sculptured decoration and numerous works of religious art.

The **Puerta del Reloj** (Clock Doorway), in the north wall, is the old entrance, dating from the 13C although modified in the 19C.

The **main façade** is pierced by three tall 15C portals of which the upper registers were completed in the 16C and 17C. At the centre is the **Puerta del Perdón** (Pardon Doorway), crowned with a tympanum illustrating the legend according to which the Virgin Mary, wishing to reward San Ildefonso for his devotion, appeared, at Assumption. The harmonious tower is 15C; the dome, which replaces the second tower, was designed by El Greco's son in the 17C.

TOLEDO

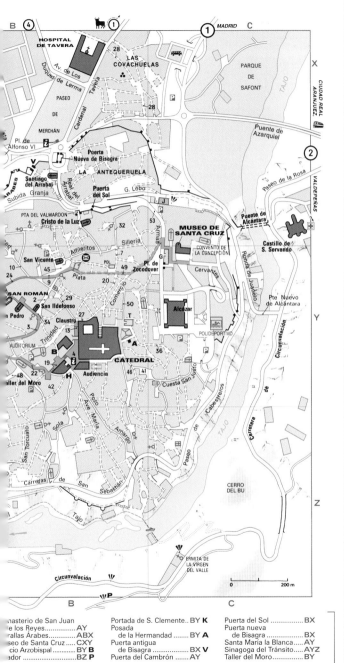

J. Malburet/MICHELIN

Cathedral

In the south wall, the 15C **Puerta de los Leones** (Lion Doorway) designed by Master Hanequin of Brussels and Juan Alemán was flanked in 1800 by a neo-Classical portal.

Enter through the Puerta del Mollete, left of the west front, which opens onto the cloisters.

The size and sturdy character of the cathedral rather than its elevation are what strike one as one gazes up over the five unequal aisles and the great supporting pillars. A wonderful collection of stained glass (1418-1561) colours the windows; magnificent wrought-iron grilles enclose the chancel, *coro* and chapels. The attention is also drawn to the cardinals' hats hanging from the vaults above the tombs of those cardinals who were primates of Spain.

Capilla Mayor – The chancel, the most sumptuous part of the cathedral, was enlarged in the 16C by Cardinal Cisneros.

The immense polychrome **retable****, carved in Flamboyant style with the Life of Christ depicted in detail on five registers, is awe inspiring. The silver statue of the Virgin at the predella dates from 1418. The marble tomb of Cardinal Mendoza in Plateresque style on the left is by Covarrubias. The recumbent figure is the work of an Italian artist.

Coro – A series of 14C high reliefs and wrought-iron enclosed chapels form the perimeter of the choir which is itself closed by an elegant iron screen (1547).

Within are magnificent 15C and 16C **choir stalls***** of which the lower parts, in wood, were carved by Rodrigo Alemán to recall, in 54 picturesque scenes, the conquest of Granada; the 16C upper parts, in alabaster are by Berruguete *(left)* and Felipe Vigarny *(right)*. The central low relief, the Transfiguration, is also by Berruguete. The style of his work creates the impression

of movement while that of Vigarny is more static. The pipes of a sonorous organ dominate the central area, occupied by two bronze lecterns and a Gothic eagle lectern. The 14C marble White Virgin is French.

Girola – The double ambulatory, surmounted by an elegant triforium with multifoil arches, is bordered by seven apsidal chapels separated by small square chapels.

There is little room to step back for a good look at the **Transparente***, the contentious but famous work by Narciso Tomé which forms a Baroque island in the Gothic church. Illuminated by the sun's rays which pour through

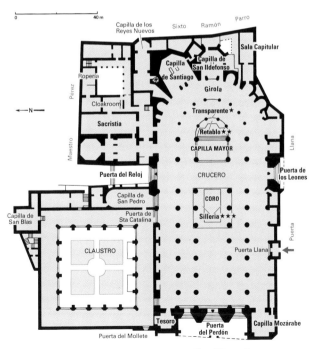

Plaza del Ayuntamiento

an opening in the ambulatory roof (made to allow light to fall on the tabernacle), the Transparente appears as an ornamental framework of angels and swirling clouds and rays surrounding the Virgin and the Last Supper.

The **Capilla de San Ildefonso** (Chapel of San Ildefonso) contains tombs, of which the one in the centre, of Cardinal Gil de Albornoz (14C), is the most notable.

The **Capilla de Santiago** (St James) is a mausoleum for Don Álvaro de Luna, Constable of Castilla, and his family.

Sala Capitular (Chapter house) – The antechamber is adorned with an impressive Mudéjar ceiling and two carved walnut wardrobes. Remarkable Mudéjar stucco doorways and carved Plateresque panels precede the chapter house where there is a particularly beautiful multicoloured **Mudéjar ceiling***. Below the frescoes by Juan de Borgoña, are portraits of former archbishops including two by Goya painted in 1804 and 1823.

Sacristía (Sacristy) – The first gallery, with its vaulted ceiling painted by Lucas Jordán, includes a powerful group of **paintings by El Greco*** of which **El Expolio** (the Saviour stripped of His Raiment) is outstanding. Also among the collection is one of El Greco's series of portraits of the Apostles. Works by other artists in the sacristy include a remark-

able portrait of *Pope Paul III* by Titian, a *Holy Family* by Van Dyck, a *Mater Dolorosa* by Morales and the *Taking of Christ* by Goya. There is also one of Pedro de Mena's (17C), *St Francis of Assisi* (in a glass case).

In the vestry are portraits by Velázquez *(Cardinal Borja)*, Van Dyck *(Pope Innocent XI)* and Ribera. The old laundry *(ropería)* contains liturgical objects. Continuing on from the sacristy you reach the **Nuevas Salas del Museo Catedralicio** (Cathedral Museum's New Galleries), installed in the Casa del Tesorero (Treasurer's House). The rooms display works by Caravaggio, El Greco, Bellini and Morales.

Tesoro (Treasury) – A Plateresque doorway by Covarrubias opens into the chapel under the tower. Beneath a Granada style Mudéjar ceiling note the splendid 16C silver-gilt **monstrance*** by Enrique de Arfe, which, although it weighs 180kg and is 3m high (just under 400lb and 10ft high), is paraded through the streets at Corpus Christi. The pyx at its centre is fashioned from gold brought from America by Christopher Columbus.

There is also a 13C Bible given by St Louis of France to St Ferdinand (Ferdinand III of Castilla).

Capilla Mozárabe (Mozarabic Chapel) – The chapel beneath the dome was built by Cardinal Cisneros (16C) to celebrate Mass according to the Visigothic or Mozarabic ritual which had been threatened with abolition in the 11C.

Claustro (Cloisters) – The architectural simplicity of the 14C lower gallery contrasts with the bold mural decoration by Bayeu of the Lives of Toledan saints (Santa Eugenia and San Ildefonso).

Iglesia de Santo Tomé

☏ 925 25 12 32. The church has a distinctive 14C Mudéjar tower. Inside is El Greco's famous painting *The Burial of the Count of Orgaz**** executed for the church in about 1586. The interment is transformed by the miraculous appearance of St Augustine and St Stephen waiting to welcome the figure from earth, symbolised by a frieze of figures in which, as he highlighted faces and hands and painted vestments with detailed biblical references, El Greco made every man an individual portrait – he is said to have painted a self-portrait in the sixth figure from the left.

Casa y Museo de El Greco* (El Greco House and Museum)

☏ 925 22 40 46.

In 1585, El Greco moved into a house similar to this attractive 16C Toledan **house**. In the first floor studio hang a *St Peter Repentant*, a version of the painting in the cathedral and, in what would have been the

El Greco House and Museum

El Greco

Domenikos Theotokopoulos, the Greek – El Greco – one of the great figures in Spanish painting, was born in Crete in 1541. After an apprenticeship painting icons, he went to Italy where he worked under Titian and studied Michelangelo before settling in Toledo in 1577 where he remained until he died in 1614. Although he did not always succeed in pleasing Philip II he found favour and fortune with Toledans. His work, with its acquired Italian techniques, retained considerable Byzantine influence which appeared as a lengthening of forms – a mannerism which increased as the painter aged.

The supernatural is a constant preoccupation, figures convey an intense spiritual inner power – all is seen with the eye of the visionary and portrayed sometimes by means of apparent distortion, by brilliant, occasionally crude colours, often by violent, swirling movement so that some pictures have the aspect of hallucinations.

artist's workroom, a signed *St Francis and Brother León*.

Museo – On the first floor of the museum are an interesting *View and Plan of Toledo* (including a likeness of his son, one with various differences from the version in the Prado) and the complete series of individual portraits of the Apostles and Christ (a later, more mature series than that in the cathedral).

The **capilla** on the ground floor, with a multicoloured Mudéjar ceiling, has a picture in the altarpiece of *St Bernardino of Siena* by El Greco. *The Crowning of Thorns* is Hispano-Flemish.

Sinagoga del Tránsito**

☏ 925 22 36 65.

Of the 10 synagogues in the old Jewish quarter (Judería), this and Santa María la Blanca are the only ones to remain. Money for its construction was provided in the 14C by Samuel Ha-Levi, treasurer to King Peter the Cruel. In 1492 it was converted into a church.

It appears from the outside as a small unpretentious building but inside, an amazing **Mudéjar decoration**** covers the upper part of the walls and all the east end. Above the rectangular hall is an *artesonado* ceiling of cedarwood; just below, are 54 multifoil arches, some blind, others pierced with delicate stone tracery. Below again runs a frieze, decorated at the east end with *mocárabes* and on the walls, bearing the arms of Castilla, with inscriptions in Hebrew.

The three arches at the centre of the east wall are surmounted by a panel in relief of roses surrounded by magnificent strapwork and, at either side, by inscriptions describing the synagogue's foundation. The women's balcony opens from the south wall.

The adjoining rooms, which had previously served as part of a Calatrava monastery, have been converted into a **Museo Sefardí** (Sephardic Museum) displaying tombs, robes, costumes and books. Several are presents from Sephardim or descendants of the Jews expelled from Spain in 1492.

Sinagoga de Santa María la Blanca★

☎ 925 22 72 57. This was the principal synagogue in Toledo in the late 12C; in 1405, however, it was given to the Knights of Calatrava who converted it into a church. Subsequent vicissitudes, the hall appears as before with five tiered aisles, separated by 24 octagonal pillars supporting horseshoe-shaped arches. The plain white of the pillars and arches is relieved by the intricately carved **capitals**★ adorned with pine cones and strapwork. The polychrome wood altarpiece is 16C.

Monasterio de San Juan de los Reyes★ (St John of the Kings Monastery)

☎ 925 22 38 02. The monastery was built by the Catholic Monarchs in thanksgiving to God for their decisive victory over the Portuguese at Toro in 1476. The overall architecture is typically Isabelline, that style which includes in the Flamboyant Gothic style touches of Mudéjar and even Renaissance art, particularly in this case since construction continued until the early 17C. The exterior is somewhat austere despite the ornamental pinnacles and stone balustrade which crown the edifice and, in the latter instance, circles the octagonal lantern. Covarrubias designed the north portal during the later stages of construction, including in the decoration the figure of John the Baptist flanked by Franciscan saints.

The fetters from the façade were taken from Christian prisoners freed from the Muslims in Andalucía.

Claustro – Although restored, the cloisters remain extremely attractive with Flamboyant bays and the original Plateresque upper galleries (1504) crowned with a pinnacled balustrade. The upper gallery has Mudéjar *artesonado* vaulting.

Iglesia – The church, rebuilt after being fired by the French in 1808, has the single wide aisle typical of Isabelline churches; at the crossing are a dome and a lantern. The **sculptured decoration**★ by the church's Flemish architect, Juan Guas, provides a delicate stone tracery *(crestería)* which at the transept forms twin tribunes for Ferdinand and Isabel. The transept walls are faced with a wonderful frieze of royal escutcheons, supported by an eagle, the symbol of St John. Other decoration includes Mudéjar *mocárabes* on the bosses in the transept vaulting and heads in picturesque high relief on the triumphal arches. The original altarpiece has been replaced by a 16C Plateresque retable. Not far away are a Visigothic palace and gateway, which were once part of the town perimeter. The gateway was rebuilt in the 16C. The **Puerta del Cambrón** is named after the *cambroneras* or hawthorns which once grew around it.

Turn left out of calle Santo Tomé onto the picturesque Travesía de Campana alley.

Before you, in the small shaded plaza del Padre Mariana, stands the monumental Baroque façade of the **Iglesia de San Ildefonso** and higher up, that of the **Iglesia de San Pedro.**

Iglesia de San Román: Museo de los Concilios de Toledo y de la Cultura Visigoda*
(Museum of the Councils of Toledo and Visigothic Culture)
☎ 925 22 78 72. The 13C Mudéjar church, at the highest point in the town, has a fine upstanding tower closely resembling that of Santo Tomé. Inside, the three aisles divided by horseshoe-shaped arches are reminiscent of Santa María la Blanca. The walls are covered in 13C frescoes of the raising of the dead, the Evangelists and, on the far wall, one of the Councils of Toledo. The apse was modified in the 16C when a cupola was built over it by Covarrubias. Note the 18C **altarpiece**.

The Visigothic collections include, in glass cases, fine bronze jewellery and copies of votive crowns decorated with cabochon stones from Guarrazar (originals in the Museo Arqueológico, Madrid).

On the walls are steles, fragments from capitals, balustrades from the choir and pilasters decorated with geometric motifs or scrollwork.

The Plateresque **doorway** (portada) opposite the church belongs to the Convento de San Clemente.

In plaza de San Vicente, note the Mudéjar east end of the **Iglesia de San Vicente** before continuing up calle de la Plata with its houses with carved entrances.

Plaza de Zocodover
This bustling triangular square is the heart of Toledo. It was rebuilt after the Civil War as was the Arco de la Sangre (Arch of Blood).

Museo de Santa Cruz**
(Santa Cruz Museum)
☎ 925 22 10 36.
This is a fine group of Plateresque buildings begun by Enrique Egas and completed by Covarrubias who was responsible for the **façade****. On the gateway tympanum Cardinal Mendoza kneels before the Cross supported by St Helena, St Peter, St Paul and two pages; on the arches are the cardinal virtues while above, two windows frame a high relief of St Joachim and St Anne.

The museum is known for its **collection of 16C and 17C pictures*** which includes **18 paintings by El Greco***. Inside, the architecture is outstanding for the size of the nave and transept – forming a two-tiered Greek cross – and for the beautiful coffered ceilings.

Ground floor – The first part of the nave contains 16C Flemish tapestries, **Primitive paintings***, and the *Astrolabios* or *Zodiac* tapestry, woven in Flanders in the mid-15C for Toledo cathedral, which fascinates still by its originality and modern colouring.

Museo de Santa Cruz, detail

Note, in the south transept, the *Ascension* and the *Presentation of Mary in the Temple* by the Maestro de Sijena. In the second part of the nave hangs the immense pennant flown by Don Juan of Austria at the Battle of Lepanto. Before it is a 17C Crucifix, recalling the one believed to have been present at the battle and which is now in Barcelona Cathedral. The north transept contains a *Christ at the Column* by Morales.

First floor – A staircase leads to the upper gallery of the north transept which displays the **paintings by El Greco★**. There are gentle portraits of the *Virgin* and *St Veronica* as well as a version of the *Expolio (original in the Cathedral Sacristy)*, later than that in the cathedral. The most famous painting in the collection is the **Altarpiece of the Assumption★**, which dates from 1613, the artist's final period. The figures are particularly elongated, the colours rasping.

The south transept contains a *Holy Family at Nazareth* by Ribera, the specialist in tenebrism (term applied to paintings in dark tones) who here showed himself to be a master of light and delicacy.

In the first part of the nave are 16C Brussels tapestries illustrating the life of Alexander the Great. There are also 17C statues from the studio of Pascual de Mena of a *Mater Dolorosa* and an *Ecce Homo*.

The **Plateresque patio★** has bays with elegant lines complemented by the openwork of the balustrade and enhanced by beautiful Mudéjar vaulting and, even more, by the magnificent **staircase★** by Covarrubias. Adjoining rooms house a museum of archaeology and decorative arts.

HIGHLIGHTS WITHIN THE CITY WALLS

Alcázar

☎ *925 22 16 73*. The Alcázar, destroyed and rebuilt so many times, stands massive and proud as ever, dominating all other buildings. It was Emperor Charles V who decided to convert the 13C fortress of which El Cid had been the first governor, into an imperial residence. The conversion was entrusted first to Covarrubias (1538-51) and subsequently to Herrera, who designed the austere south front. The siege and shelling of 1936 left the fortress in ruins.

Reconstruction has restored the Alcázar to its appearance at the time of Charles V – an innovation is the Victory Monument by Ávalos in the forecourt. Inside, you see the underground galleries which sheltered the cadets' families, and the office above in which Colonel Moscardó was ordered by phone to surrender or see his son shot. His son died on 23 August; the Alcázar was relieved on 27 September.

Weapons and uniforms are displayed in museum rooms off the patio.

buret/MICHELIN

Puerta Nueva de Bisagra

Posada de la Hermandad (House of the Brotherhood)

This 15C building used to be a prison.

Puerta del Sol

The Sun Gate in the town's second perimeter, rebuilt in the 14C, is a fine Mudéjar construction with two circumscribing horseshoe arches. At the centre a later low relief shows the Virgin presenting San Ildefonso with a chasuble. At the top, the brick decoration of blind arcading incorporates an unusual sculpture of two girls bearing the head of the chief *alguacil* (officer of justice) of the town on a salver; the story goes that he had been condemned for raping them.

Cristo de la Luz (Christ of the Light)

In AD 1000 the Moors built a mosque on the site of a ruined Visigothic church; in the 12C this mosque was converted into a Mudéjar church. Legend has it that the church was named Christ of the Light because when Alfonso VI was making his entry into Toledo, El Cid's horse in the royal train suddenly knelt before the mosque in which, within a wall, a Visigothic lamp was discovered lighting up a Crucifix. Three series of arches of different periods, intersecting blind arcades, and a line of horizontal brickwork surmounted by Cufic characters make up the façade.

The adjoining gardens lead to the top of the Puerta del Sol from which there is an interesting view of the city.

Iglesia de Santiago del Arrabal (St James on the Outskirts)

This beautifully restored Mudéjar church contains the ornate Gothic Mudéjar pulpit from which San Vicente Ferrer is said to have preached. The altarpiece is 16C.

Puerta Nueva de Bisagra (New Bisagra Gate)

The gate was rebuilt by Covarrubias in 1550 and enlarged during the reign of Philip II. Massive round crenellated towers, facing the Madrid road, flank a giant imperial crest.

Puerta Antigua de Bisagra (Old Bisagra Gate)

This gate in the former Moorish ramparts is the one through which Alfonso VI entered the city in 1085.

Taller del Moro
☏ 925 22 45 00.

This workshop (taller), used by a Moor as a collecting yard for building material for the cathedral, is in fact an old palace.

The Mudéjar decoration can still be seen in some of the rooms.

OUTSIDE THE CITY WALLS

Hospital de Tavera*
☏ 925 22 04 51.

The hospital, founded in the 16C by Cardinal Tavera, was begun by Bustamante in 1541 and completed by González de Lara and the Vergaras in the 17C. After the Civil War, the Duchess of Lerma rearranged certain apartments* in 17C style, where paintings of great artistic value may be seen.

Ground floor – The vast library contains the hospital archives. Among the paintings displayed, El Greco's Holy Family is arresting, the portrait of the Virgin perhaps the most beautiful the artist ever painted. Note also the Birth of the Messiah by Tintoretto, the Philosopher by Ribera and, in an adjoining room, his strange portrait of the Bearded Woman.

First floor – The reception hall contains another El Greco, the sombre portrait of Cardinal Tavera, painted from a death mask. Beside it are Samson and Delilah by Caravaggio and two portraits of the Duke and Duchess of Navas by Antonio Moro.

A gallery to the church leads off from the elegant twin patio. The Carrara marble portal is by Alonso Berruguete who also carved the tomb of Cardinal Tavera. The retable at the high altar was designed by El Greco whose last work, a Baptism of Christ* is displayed in the church. It is an outstanding painting in which the artist's use of brilliant colours and elongated figures is at its most magnificent.

Giving onto the patio is the hospital's former pharmacy, which has been restored.

Puente de Alcántara

The 13C bridge ends respectively to west and east in a Mudéjar tower and a Baroque arch. On the far side of the Tajo, behind battlemented ramparts, the restored 14C **Castillo de San Servando** (San Servando Castle), an advanced strongpoint in medieval times, can be seen.

A plaque on the town wall by the bridge recalls how **St John of the Cross** (1542-91) escaped through a window from his monastery prison nearby.

Puente de San Martín

The medieval bridge, rebuilt in the 14C following damage by floodwaters, is marked at its south end by an octagonal crenellated tower; the north end is 16C.

Cristo de la Vega

The Church of Christ of the Vega, formerly St Leocadia, stands on the site of a 7C Visigothic temple. Although considerably modified in the 18C, it still has a fine Mudéjar apse.

Hospital de Tavera

Decorative tiles in the "Los Timbales" bar

Getting About

Airport – Madrid-Barajas airport is located 13km/8mi east of the city, alongside the N II highway. A shuttle bus operates to the airport from plaza de Colón, with six pick-up points along its route. Metro line no8, which links up with line no4, connects the airport with the city.

Airport information ☎ 902 35 35 70.

Info-Iberia ☎ 902 400 500.

RENFE (Spanish State Railways) – The city's main railway stations are Atocha and Chamartín. For information and reservations, call ☎ 902 24 02 02 (24-hr information; reservations from 5.30am-11.50pm).

Madrid also has a comprehensive local train network which can be used to get to El Escorial, the Sierra de Guadarrama, Alcalá de Henares and Aranjuez.

Inter-city buses – Most buses to other cities depart from the Estación Sur, calle Méndez Álvaro. ☎ 91 468 42 00.

Taxis – Madrid has a huge number of registered taxis with their distinctive white paintwork with a red diagonal stripe on the rear doors. At night, the green light indicates that the taxi is for hire.

Local buses – For information, call ☎ 91 406 88 00. Buses provide a good opportunity to see the city, although traffic jams are a major problem. Passengers should also beware of pickpockets. Times vary from line to line, but generally buses operate between 6am and 11.30pm. Night buses operate from 11.30pm onwards, with most departing from plaza de Cibeles. In addition to single tickets, passengers can also purchase a 10-trip **Metro-bus** ticket *(un bono de 10 viajes)* valid on both the bus and metro network, as well as a zone-based monthly ticket *(bono mensual)* which is valid for an unlimited number of bus and metro journeys for one month.

Metro – *Metro stations are shown on the maps in this guide*. For information, call ☎ 902 444 403. The metro system is the fastest way to get around the city and consists of 11 lines. It operates from 6am to 1.30am.

Sightseeing

The *Guía del Ocio* (www.guiadelocio.com/madrid) is a weekly guide containing a list of every cultural event and show in the city. It can be purchased at newspaper stands.

Bus turístico Madrid Visión – This tourist bus offers three different routes around the city (historic Madrid, modern Madrid and monumental Madrid). Tickets, which can be purchased on board, in hotels or via a travel agent, are valid for 1 or 2 days. During the period of validity, passengers can hop on and off as much as they like as well as change their route. Services operate from 10am-7pm in winter, 10am-9pm in spring and autumn, and 9.30am-midnight in summer. Stops include the Puerta del Sol, plaza de Cibeles, paseo del Prado and Puerta de Alcalá. For information and prices, call ☎ 91 779 18 88.

Where to Eat

Here is a list of restaurants selected for their location, ambience or distinctive character. There are three categories.

- ⊖ Budget: under €15
- ⊖⊖ Moderate: between €15 and €30
- ⊖⊖⊜ Expensive: over €30

⊖ **La Finca de Susana** – *Arlaban 4 (Huertas)* - ⋒ *Sevilla* - ☏ *91 369 35 57* - ▤ - *€14/18.* This very popular establishment is in the centre of town. When it is crowded, there is often a long wait for service. The customers are young and cosmopolitan. It is best to arrive early. Excellent value for your money.

⊖⊖ **La Bola** – *Bola 5 (Centro)* – ⋒ *Ópera* – ☏ *91 547 69 30* – *Closed Sun evening* – ⌿ ▤ – *€22/30.* If you're hoping to try a traditional *cocido madrileño*, look no further than this famous tavern which has been serving up this traditional dish in earthenware pots for over a century.

⊖⊖ **La Vaca Verónica** – *Moratín 38 (Huertas)* - ☏ *91 429 78 27* - *Closed Sat lunchtime* - ▤ - *€23.50/28.* In this warm and welcoming restaurant, you can enjoy very good grilled meats and a delicious pasta and shrimp dish, "pasta con carabineros".

⊖⊖ **Teatriz** – *Hermosilla 15 (Salamanca)* - ⋒ *Serrano* - ☏ *91 577 53 79* - ▤ - *€24.90/35.80.* Designed by Philippe Starck, this former theatre has been converted into an impressive-looking restaurant where you can choose between eating in the orchestra or enjoying a drink at the stage bar. The good, reasonably priced menu is based around Mediterranean dishes and Italian specialities.

⊖⊖ **Zerain** – *Quevedo 3 (Huertas)* - ⋒ *Antón Martín* - ☏ *91 429 79 09* - *Closed Holy Week, Aug and Sun* - ▤ - *€25.50/31.* One of the typical menus at this Basque cider bar near plaza de Santa Ana includes *tortilla de bacalao* (cod omelette) and *chuletón* (meat cutlets). Rustic, but pleasant decor. The cider here is served directly from the barrel.

⊖⊖ **Casa Lucio** – *Cava Baja 35 (La Latina)* - ⋒ *La Latina* - ☏ *91 365 32 52* - *Closed Sat lunchtime and Aug* - *€30/40.* One of Madrid's best-known addresses, Casa Lucio is frequented by politicians, actors and visitors alike. Typical Castilian decor. Famous for its *huevos estrellados* (fried eggs).

⊖⊖⊜ **El Amparo** – *Puigcerdá 8 (Salamanca)* - ⋒ *Retiro* - ☏ *91 431 64 56* - *Cerrado sá mediodía, do y Sem Santa* - ▤ - *60/67€.* This luxurious restaurant is decorated with unique style – the dining rooms are on several levels, the mansard roof is fitted with skylights – and the service is excellent. Very pleasant ambience. The cuisine is refined and the prices reflect this.

In Alcalá de Henares

⊖⊖⊜ **Miguel de Cervantes** – *Imagen 12* - ☏ *91 883 12 77* - ▤ - *€30.75/ 37.75.* This restaurant, well-located behind Cervantes' birthplace, is housed in a restored town house and serves traditional cuisine against a backdrop of typical Castilian decor. A few reasonably priced rooms are also available.

In Segovia

⊖⊖ **Narizotas** – *Plaza de Medina del Campo 1* - ☏ *921 46 26 79* - *€16/26.* In this traditional restaurant, customers can choose between the classic roast suckling-pig *(cochinillo asado)* or a more original menu comprising specialities such as local sausages *(embutidos)* and fricassée of lamb *(cochifrito)*. During the summer, there's also the option of eating on the pleasant street terrace.

⊖⊖ **Mesón de Cándido** – *Plaza Azoguejo 5 -* ☎ *921 42 59 11 -* ▤ *-* *€23.40/28.30*. This is surely the most famous restaurant in the whole province. At the foot of the aqueduct, in a 15C house decorated country-style, you can enjoy a tasty suckling-pig, the house speciality.

In Toledo

⊖ **La Abadía** – *Plaza de San Nicolás 3 -* ☎ *925 25 11 40 - €10.70/26*. The owners of this restaurant have successfully transformed the basement of this former 16C palace. The complex lighting and modern furniture combine to create a highly original overall effect and a pleasant backdrop to some creative cuisine. Not for those suffering from claustrophobia.

⊖⊖ **Casón de los López de Toledo** – *Sillería 3 -* ☎ *925 25 47 74 -* *Closed Sun Evening -* ▤ *-* *€24/43€*. Time seems to have stood still in this stone mansion built around a fountain-adorned patio. A delightful setting in which to try local specialities such as partridge stew *(perdiz estofada)* and wild boar *(jabali)*. The bar on the ground floor serves a range of tapas.

𝒯apas

In tapas bars, prices are not listed. Tapas and raciones vary from one place to another, but as a general rule you should be able to have a reasonably good meal for under €15.

Casa Labra – *Tetuán 12 (Centro) -* ▲ *Sol -* ☎ *91 531 00 81*. This old tavern dating back to the middle of the 19C is a Madrid institution. It was here that Pablo Iglesias founded the Spanish Socialist Party (PSOE) in 1879. Its house speciality is fried cod *(bacalao frito),* which you can enjoy standing up on the street or at the marble tables inside.

Taberna Almendro 13 – *Almendro 13 (La Latina) -* ▲ *La Latina -* ☎ *91 365 42 52 -* ⊐ ▤. Although it has only been in business for 8 years, this new tavern with an old atmosphere is always packed. Its tapas include cheese and sausage pastries *(roscas de queso y embutido)*, fried eggs *(huevos estrellados)* and its potato-based *patatas emporradas*.

La Venencia – *Echegaray 7 (Huertas) -* ▲ *Sevilla -* ☎ *91 429 73 13 -* ⊐. If your taste is for sherry, then this is the place for you. La Venencia is a small, narrow bar in the Huertas district which more than makes up in atmosphere and cuisine what it lacks in size. The yellowish, flaking walls and wooden bar provide added character. Cold tapas only.

Taberna de Dolores – *Pl. de Jesús 4 (Huertas) -* ▲ *Antón Martín -* ☎ *91 429 22 43 -* ⊐ ▤. *Azulejos* on the façade and a large, crowded bar on the inside are the distinctive features of this popular bar. Excellent draught beer, anchovies *(boquerones)* in vinegar, canapés etc.

Prada a Tope – *Príncipe 11 (Huertas) -* ▲ *Sevilla -* ☎ *91 429 59 21 - Closed Mon and August -* ▤ *- €8.50*. This bar is inspired by traditions from the Castilla y Léon region. The rustic decor is typical of El Bierzo area, with wood and slate prominent. The bar and tables are big, the walls covered with photographs. Sale of regional products.

Taberna de la Daniela – *General Pardiñas 21 (Salamanca)* - ☎ *Goya* - ☏ *91 575 23 29* - ▤ - *€5*. A new bar with traditional-style decoration. *Azulejos* on the outside with vermouth on tap and a wide selection of canapés and *raciones* inside. Specialities here include *cocido madrileño*.

José Luis – *Serrano 89 (Salamanca)* - ☎ *Núñez de Balboa* - ☏ *91 563 09 58* - ▤ - *€15*. A Salamanca institution. In two parts, each with its distinct style, but sharing the same bar. A wide choice of superb tapas; its Spanish omelette is the most famous in the city. Tables outside in summer.

))) here to Stay

Our selection of hotels is divided into three categories, based on tax-exclusive prices for a private room. All of them were chosen for location, comfort, the value for money and, in some cases, for their unique charm. The two prices that are given correspond to a single room off-season and a double room in high season.

- ⊝ Budget: rooms under €55
- ⊝⊝ Moderate: rooms between €50 and €80
- ⊝⊝⊝ Expensive: more than €80

⊝ **Hostal Miguel Ángel** – *San Mateo 21 2ºD (Bilbao)* - ☎ *Tribunal* - ☏ *91 447 54 00* - *16 rooms. €45/60.* Next to the Museo Romántico. The somewhat darkened brick conceals a well-maintained hotel with a fabulous wooden staircase leading to the reception on the second floor. Friendly staff and spotless, more than adequate rooms with TV and en-suite bathroom.

⊝ **Hotel Centro Sol** – *Carrrera de San Jerónimo 5, 2º-4º (Centro)* - ☎ *Sol* - ☏ *91 522 15 82* - ▤ - *35 rooms. €46/55 (including VAT).* A hotel very close to the Puerta del Sol occupying the second and fourth floors of a building somewhat lacking in charm. However, its rooms, all with TVs and good bathrooms, are very reasonably priced and have been recently refurbished.

⊝ **Hotel Plaza Mayor** – *Atocha 2 (Centro)* - ☎ *Sol* - ☏ *91 360 06 06* - ▤ - *31rooms. €48/70* - ▭ *€3.50.* An unpretentious hotel, but with a great location right by the city's main square. Behind the modern brick façade, the rooms are small, functional but attractively decorated.

⊝⊝ **Hotel Mora** – *Paseo del Prado 32 (Retiro)* - ☎ *Atocha* - ☏ *91 420 15 69* - *60 rooms €57/75 (including VAT).* The Mora enjoys a superb location in an impressive building opposite the botanical gardens on paseo del Prado. Comfortable, recently renovated rooms and reasonable rates.

⊝⊝ **Hotel Inglés** – *Echegaray 8 (Centro)* - ☎ *Sevilla* - ☏ *91 429 65 51* - *58 rooms.* €70/100 - ▭ *€5.* There's no doubting the character of this hotel built in 1853. A good central and moderately priced option in the Chueca distrct, an area renowned for its lively nightlife. Clean, comfortable rooms.

⊝⊝ **Hotel París** – *Alcalá 2 (Centro)* - ☎ *Sol* - ☏ *91 521 64 96* - *120 rooms.* €70/90 (including VAT) ▭. At the time it was built (1863) the París was one of the most elegant and prestigious hotels in the city. Today, it is one of the oldest in Madrid and despite losing some of its former splendour still retains its old-world charm. Large, adequate rooms, albeit on the antiquated side.

Hotel La Residencia de El Viso – *Nervión 8 (República Argentina) - República Argentina - ☎ 91 564 03 70 - ▦ - 12 rooms. €76/127 - €⌣ 9 - Restaurant €30.80/56.40.* This small hotel occupies an early-20C mansion in a residential area near plaza de la República Argentina. Elegant decor and a charming patio.

Hotel Casón del Tormes – *Río 7 (Centro) - Plaza de España - ☎ 91 541 97 46 - ▦ - 63 rooms. €79/97 - €⌣ 6.50.* Located in a small, quiet street in the centre of the city, just behind the Senate building. Built in the middle of the 1960s, the hotel has large, comfortable rooms which have been recently renovated.

Hotel Carlos V – *Maestro Vitoria 5 (Centro) - Sol - ☎ 91 531 41 00 - ▦ - 67 rooms. from €98.50 ⌣.* A good central option in a pedestrianised street away from the noise of the city. Although small, the English-style rooms are pleasant and well appointed. An eclectic cafeteria on the first floor.

Hotel Ritz – *Plaza de la Lealtad 5 (Retiro) - Banco de España - ☎ 91 701 67 67 - ▦ 占 - 137 rooms. from €560 - ⌣ €30 - Restaurant €62/79.* A magnificent early-20C building superbly located near paseo del Prado. The hotel has all the elegance, tradition and comfort you would expect from such a famous name, plus prices to match. The terrace-garden here is an additional delight.

In Segovia

Hotel Don Jaime – *Ochoa Ondátegui 8 - ☎ 921 44 47 90 - 16 rooms. €22/40 - ⌣ €3.* The bedrooms in this welcoming Castilian mansion, magnificently located at the foot of the Roman aqueduct, are simple, bright and quiet.

Hotel Las Sirenas – *Juan Bravo 30 - ☎ 921 46 26 63 - ▦ - 39 rooms. €53/70.* This hotel from another age, at the heart of Segovia's old quarter, has an elegant stone façade and rooms that are comfortable, albeit lacking in luxuries. The attractive staircase and old hairdressing salon are reminders of its better days.

In Toledo

Hotel La Almazara – *3.5km/2mi SW along the Cuerva road - ☎ 925 22 38 66 - Open Mar-10 Dec. - ▣ - Reservation recommended - 28 rooms. €28/39 - ⌣ €3.50.* This former cardinal's residence is reached via a lane planted with olive trees. The building's sturdy walls are clad with ivy, while the bedrooms are spacious and bright, some with terrace in the shade of magnificent gardens.

Hostal del Cardenal – *Paseo Recaredo 24 - ☎ 925 22 49 00 - ▦ - 27 rooms. €60.13/96.93 - ⌣ €6.90 - Restaurant €23.24/36.25.* This charming hotel, half-hidden in a delighful garden full of fountains, low walls and flowers, stands at the foot of the city walls. Behind the splendid stone façade, the bedrooms are elegantly decorated with wood furnishings and antiques. The restaurant here is superb.

Bars and Cafés

Café de Oriente – *plaza Oriente 2 -* ⌖ *Ópera -* ☎ *91 5 41 39 74 - Open 8.30am-2am.* This classic institution, located in the plaza de Oriente opposite the Royal Palace, is a delightful place for a drink at any time of day. Pleasant terrace.

Café del Círculo de Bellas Artes – *Marqués de Casa Riera 2 -* ⌖ *Banco de España, Sevilla -* ☎ *91 3 60 54 00 - Open Mon-Thu and Sun 9am-midnight, Fri-Sat 9am-3am.* The marked 19C atmosphere of this great café with its enormous columns and large windows is in sharp contrast to its young, intellectual clientele. Outdoor terrace in summer. Highly recommended.

El Espejo – *Paseo de Recoletos 21 -* ⌖ *Colón -* ☎ *913 19 11 22 - Open 9am-2am.* An attractive, Modernist-style café close to the Café Gijón (below) with a charming wrought-iron and glass canopy.

Café Gijón – *Paseo de Recoletos 31 -* ⌖ *Banco de España -* ☎ *91 5 21 54 25 - Open 7am-2am.* This café, which has long been famous as a meeting point for artists and writers, continues the tradition to this day. Outdoor terrace in summer.

Café Central – *plaza del Ángel 10 -* ⌖ *Antón Martín -* ☎ *91 3 69 41 43 - Abre 14-3.30. Open 2pm-3.30am.* One of the city's main haunts for jazz-lovers since the early 1980s.

Los Gabrieles – *Echegaray 17 -* ⌖ *Sevilla -* ☎ *91 429 62 61 - Open Mon-Thu 12.30pm-2am, Fri-Sat 12.30pm-3.30am.* Tapas by day and a bar by night. A favourite haunt for foreign students in Madrid, attracted, no doubt, by the historical chronicles on its *azulejo*-decorated panelling.

Irish Rover – *avenida de Brasil 7 -* ⌖ *Santiago Bernabeu -* ☎ *91 5 55 76 71 - Open Mon-Thu and Sun 11am-2.30pm and Fri-Sat 11am-3.30am.* A pub within a pub. A section which looks as though it has come straight out of one of Joyce's novels and a tiny lounge are just two of the features of this Irish home-from-home. Daily performances and a small market on Sundays. Young clientele.

Joy Eslava – *Arenal 11 -* ⌖ *Ópera, Sol -* ☎ *913 66 37 33 - Open Mon-Thu 11.30pm-5am, Fri-Sat 11.30pm-6am.* This well-known club, occupying a former 19C theatre, has been attracting a colourful crowd of club-goers and famous faces for several decades. On your way home, why not pay a visit to the famous Chocolatería de San Ginés, in the street of the same name.

Libertad, 8 – *Libertad 8 -* ⌖ *Chueca -* ☎ *9 15 32 73 48 - Open 1am-4am.* A building over a century old is the setting for this atmospheric café, renowned for its poetry readings and storytellers, attracting young, bohemian audiences.

Palacio de Gaviria – *Arenal 9 -* ⌖ *Sol -* ☎ *91 5 26 60 69 - Open Sun-Wed 8pm-3am, Fri-Sat 11pm-6am.* A fascinating club which has been converted from one of Madrid's old palaces. Also famous for its ballroom dancing. Its Thursday-night *fiesta internacional* is very popular with foreigners.

Del Diego – *La Reina 12 -* ⌖ *Gran Vía -* ☎ *91 5 23 31 06 - Open Mon-Thu 7pm-3am, Fri-Sat 7pm-4am.* A pleasant bar serving some of the city's best cocktails.

Entertainment

Madrid has over 100 cinemas, including one **Imax** cinema, 20 or so theatres, numerous concert halls and one casino. The **Auditorio Nacional** (opened in 1988) has a varied programme of classical music, the **Teatro de la Zarzuela** hosts a wide range of shows including Spanish operettas *(zarzuelas)* and ballets, while the **Teatro Real** offers a season of opera. The **Veranos de la Villa** and the **Festival de Otoño** are two events held in the summer and autumn respectively with an interesting mix of cultural performances. The **Festival Internacional de Jazz** is another event also held during November.

Berlín Cabaret – *Costanilla de San Pedro 11 – ⊙ La Latina – Open Mon-Thu and Sun, 11pm-5am and Fri-Sat, 11pm-6am.* One of Madrid's famous venues. Live acts (magicians, drag queens etc) and a fun atmosphere.

Café de Chinitas – *Torija 7 - ⊙ Callao - ☎ 91 5 47 15 02 - Open Mon-Sat, 10.30pm-5am.* Very popular with tourists. Dinner shows also available.

Casa Patas – *Cañizares 10 - ⊙ Antón Martín - ☎ 91 3 69 04 96 - Open Mon-Sun, noon-5pm; Fri-Sat, 8pm-2.30am and Sun-Thu, 8pm-1.30am.* One of the best venues in which to enjoy a night of flamenco.

Zarzu

Shopping

Casa Mira – *Carrera San Jerónimo 30 - ⋒ Sevilla - ☏ 91 429 88 95 - Open 10am-2pm, 5pm-9pm.* The best sweets in town (turrón, marzipan, …). The Casa Mira is a veritable institution, run by the same family since 1842. The products for sale are all of "suprema" quality, without preservatives or additives, weighed and cut before the customer's hungry eye.

La Violeta – *Plaza de Canalejas 6 - ⋒ Sevilla - ☏ 91 522 55 22 – Closed Aug, Sun and holidays – 9.30am-2pm, 4.30-8.30pm.* In business since 1915, this confectioner known for his delicious sweets boasts an illustrious list of clients past and present, including King Alphonse XIII, Jacinto Benavente and Valle Inclán. The chocolate and the violet-flavoured sweets are favourites, along with the glazed chestnuts.

Capas Seseña – *Cruz 23 (Huertas) - ⋒ Sevilla o Sol - ☏ 91 531 68 40 - www.sesena.com – 10am-1.30pm, 4.30-8pm.* This family business, founded in 1901, provides its customers with tailor-made capes, both classic and modern, made with the very finest fabrics. There are a few photographs of celebrities who have enjoyed wearing their attire: Hemingway, Picasso, Catherine Deneuve, Rudolf Valentino, Marcelo Mastroianni, ….

Art Galleries – A number of galleries can be found in and around Atocha, close to the Centro de Arte Reina Sofía, in the Salamanca district (near the Puerta de Alcalá) and on the left side of the paseo de la Castellana, close to the calle Génova.

In Toledo

Toledo is renowned for its **damascene ware** (black steel inlaid with gold, silver and copper thread) as well as its culinary specialities including braised partridge and marzipan.

Fiestas

On 15 May, the city commemorates the feast day of **San Isidro**, its patron saint. The day is celebrated in a variety of ways: an outdoor picnic, impromptu dancing, rock concerts and above all through its famous bullfighting festival, which lasts for some six weeks. It is also traditional for *madrileños* to eat traditional pastries *(rosquillas)* on this special day.

In Aranjuez

The colourful **Ferias del Motín**, in which hundreds of participants dressed in period costume re-enact the famous revolt which took place in Aranjuez, is held during the first week of September.

In Toledo

Toledo's streets provide a splendid setting for the **Corpus Christi** procession, one of the largest in Spain, held on the first Sunday following Corpus Christi.

*I*ndex

Director	David Brabis
Series Editor	Ana González
Editorial team	Grace Coston, Blandine Lecomte
Picture Editor	Alexandra Rosina
Mapping	Michèle Cana, Daniel Duguay
Graphic Coordination	Marie-Pierre Renier, Marc Pinard
Graphics	Jean-Luc Cannet
Typesetting	Jean-Paul Josset
Production	Renaud Leblanc
Marketing	Ellie Danby
Sales	John Lewis (UK), Robin Bird (USA)

Manufacture Française des Pneumatiques MICHELIN
Société en commandite par actions au capital de 304 000 000 €
Place des Carmes-Déchaux - 63000 Clermont-Ferrand (France)
R.C.S. Clermont-Fd B 855 200 507

© Michelin et Cie, Propriétaires-éditeurs
Dépot légal mai 2005 - ISBN 2-06-711547-2
Printed in France 05-05/1.1

No part of this publication may be reproduced in any form
without the prior permission of the publisher.

Typesetting: NORD COMPO, Villeneuve-d'Ascq (France)
Printing-binding: POLLINA, Luçon (Francia) - L96120b

MICHELIN TRAVEL PUBLICATIONS
Hannay House - 39 Clarendon Road - WATFORD, WD17 1JA
☎ 01923 205240 - Fax 01923 205241
www.ViaMichelin.com - TheGreenGuide-uk@uk.michelin.com